Second Edition

Renaissance, Revolution and Reformation

Britain 1485–1750

Aaron Wilkes
James Ball

OXFORD

UNIVERSITY PRESS

OXFORD
UNIVERSITY PRESS

Great Clarendon Street, Oxford OX2 6DP

Oxford University Press is a department of the University of Oxford.
It furthers the University's objective of excellence in research,
scholarship, and education by publishing worldwide in

Oxford   New York

Auckland Cape Town Dar es Salaam Hong Kong Karachi
Kuala Lumpur Madrid Melbourne Mexico City Nairobi
New Delhi Shanghai Taipei Toronto

With offices in

Argentina Austria Brazil Chile Czech Republic France Greece
Guatemala Hungary Italy Japan Poland Portugal Singapore
South Korea Switzerland Thailand Turkey Ukraine Vietnam

Oxford is a registered trade mark of Oxford University Press
in the UK and in certain other countries

British Library Cataloguing in Publication Data

Data available

ISBN: 978-1-85008-345-0

FD3450

10 9 8 7 6 5 4

Printed in China by Printplus

Paper used in the production of this book is a natural, recyclable product
made from wood grown in sustainable forests. The manufacturing process
conforms to the environmental regulations of the country of origin.

Editors: Daniel Bottom and Joanne Mitchell
Layout artist: Sally Boothroyd
Illustrations: Jamil Dar, Tony Randell and Clive Wakfer
Cover design: Mike Cryer at EMC Design
Cover image: Mary Evans Picture Library

Acknowledgements

© 2003 TopFoto/Topham Picturepoint: 31; © 2004 Topfoto/Fotomas:
79; © 2005 TopFoto/Fotomas: 43; Archivo Iconografico, SA/Corbis:
30; Ashmolean Museum, University of Oxford, UK/Bridgeman Art
Library: 99; © Bettmann/CORBIS: 131, 134 (bottom); Bodleian Library:
133 (bottom), 143 (bottom); Bridgeman Art Library: 25, 100/101,
103; Bridgeman Art Library/Bristol City Museum & Art Gallery: 19;
Bridgeman Art Library/Gemaldegalerie, Berlin, Germany: 48 (top
right); Bridgeman Art Library/Musee de Louvre: 21 (top right);
Bridgeman Art Library/Museum of Fine Arts, Budapest: 121 (top);
Bridgeman Art Library/Kunsthistorisches Museum Vienna: 21 (top left),
53; Bridgeman Art Library/Trustees of the Bedford Estate, Woburn
Abbey: 26/27, 70 (right); Bridgeman Art Library/Wallace Collection:
113 (left); British Library: 48 (top left), 52; © British Library Board.
All Rights Reserved (H/10ff.3v): 61; British Library, Shelfmark/Man:
Add.15760. F68v-69: 38; Burghley House Collection, Lincolnshire,
UK/Bridgeman Art Library: 70 (middle); Corbis/Martin Jones: 104;
Dean Conger/Corbis: 37 (both); Dr Craig W Thornber: 29; Fortean
Picture Library: 127; Fotomas Index: 63, 95 (both), 98, 103 (bottom),
117; Gianni Dagli Orti/Corbis: 31; Joanne Mitchell: 34; Mary
Evans/Grosvenor Prints: 125; Mary Evans Picture Library: 8, 65, 69
(left), 73, 79, 80, 81, 84, 84, 85 (both), 114 (top), 124; Michael
Nicholson/Corbis: 122; Museum of London, UK/The Bridgeman Art
Library: 114 (bottom); Museum of English Rural Life: 126; National
Archives: 113 (right); National Maritime Museum, Greenwich, London:
48 (bottom left); National Portrait Gallery: 11, 14, 20 (both), 24, 39
(bottom), 35, 71 (left); National Portrait Gallery, London, UK/
Bridgeman Art Library: 71 (left); National Trust Photo Library: 46,
47 (top and bottom); Patrick Ward/Corbis: 32; Portland Gallery,
London, UK/The Bridgeman Art Library: 8/9; Private Collection,
Ken Welsh/Bridgeman Art Library: 71 (right); Private Collection/
The Bridgeman Art Library: 94; Royal Collection Enterprises Limited ©
HM Queen Elizabeth II: 39 (top), 69; Scottish National Portrait Gallery,
Edinburgh, Scotland/Bridgeman Art Library: 142; Scottish Viewpoint
Picture Library: 47 (middle); Sue Sharp: 135; TopFoto/Ann Ronan
Picture Library/HIP: 132; Topfoto/Corporation of London/HIP: 121
(bottom); Topfoto.co.uk: 134 (top); TopFoto/Fotomas: 41, 48 (bottom
right), 95, 117; The Royal Collection © 2008 HM Queen Elizabeth II:
21 (bottom), 23, 138; The Royal Collection Picture Library: 143;
Worthing Museum and Art Gallery, Sussex, UK/The Bridgeman Art
Library: 75.

'Book of Martyrs', John Fox, Ambassador Productions Ltd, 1995: 25;
'Crown and Country, Britain 1500-1750, Homework and Extension
Pack', Martyn Wiltcock and John D. Clare, Hodder, 2000: 107;
'Description of Elizabethan England 1577', William Harrison, Kessinger
Publishing Co., 2004: 42; 'History Alive 1 1485–1714', Peter Moss,
Hart-Davis Education Ltd., 1980: 24, 96, 123; 'In Search of History
1485–1714', J. F. Aylett. Hodder Arnold, 1984: 122; 'Oliver Cromwell
and His World', Maurice Ashley, Thames & Hudson, 1972: 96; 'Past
into Present 2, 1400–1700', Mary Carter, Christopher Culpin and
Nicholas Kinloch, Collins Educational, 1990: 99; Quest: 'The World
of Enlightenment, Activity Support Guide', Simon Rodden, Norman
Hobson and Bea Stimpson, Nelson Thornes, 1999: 97; SHP
'Discovering the Making of the UK', John Murray, published by Colin
Shephard and Tim Lomas, 1995: 95, 99, 101.

Contents

What is history?

Before you start this book, take a few minutes to think about these questions.

- What do you think history is? What does the word mean?
- What have you learnt in history lessons before, perhaps in your primary school? Did you enjoy them or not? If you enjoyed them, say why. If you didn't enjoy them, why not?
- Have you read any history books or stories about things that happened a long time ago? Have you watched any television programmes, films or plays about things that happened in the past? If so, which ones?

History is about what happened in the past. It is about people in the past, what they did and why they did it, what they thought and what they felt. To enjoy history you need to have a good imagination. You need to be able to imagine what life was like in the past, or what it may have been like to be involved in past events.

How did people feel, think and react to events like these?

I am Catherine Parr's best friend. She is Henry VIII's sixth wife and I have to advise her how to survive. What does he like? What does he hate? And what happened to his other five wives?

The King is very sick and I am his doctor! What treatments can I use? Which will work? Which will make him worse? What will happen to me if he dies?

I am the first Englishman to reach the mysterious land of Japan. How will these strange people treat me? Why do they think I am a savage? How and why are their lives so different?

How to use this book

As you work through this book, you will notice a number of features that keep appearing.

___ MISSION OBJECTIVES ___

All sections of this book will start by setting your Mission Objectives. These are your key aims that set out your learning targets for the work ahead. Topics will end by trying to get you to assess your own learning. If you can accomplish each Mission Objective then you are doing well!

__ MISSION ACCOMPLISHED? __

WISE-UP Words are key terms that are vital to help you discuss and understand the topics. You can spot them easily because they are in bold type. Look up their meanings in a dictionary or use the Glossary at the end of the book. The Glossary is a list of words and their meanings.

Some topics contain PAUSE for Thought boxes. This is an opportunity for you to stop and think for yourself.

▌▌ PAUSE for Thought

The Hungry for MORE features give you a chance to extend your knowledge and research beyond the classroom. This is a time for you to take responsibility for your own learning. You might be asked to research something in the library or on the Internet, work on a presentation, or design and make something. Can you meet the challenge?

✚ Hungry for **MORE**

FACT

These are all the fascinating, amazing or astounding little bits of history that you usually don't get to hear about! But in Folens History we think they are just as important and give you insights into topics that you'll easily remember.

HISTORICAL ENQUIRY

Historical Enquiries

There are also six Historical Enquiries in this book. These will get you to focus on the following themes:

- **HOW RELIGIOUS WERE THE TUDOR MONARCHS?**
- **COULD YOU GET JUSTICE IN TUDOR ENGLAND?**
- **ENGLAND ABROAD**
- **ENGLAND AT WAR**
- **HOW TOLERANT WAS CROMWELL'S COMMONWEALTH?**
- **WHO RULES?**

These themes will give you a broad knowledge of medieval religion, social attitudes and rules, power and England's relations with other countries.

Work sections are your opportunity to demonstrate your knowledge and understanding. You might be asked to put events in the correct chronological order. You might be asked to:

- explain how things have changed over time;
- work out why two people might interpret the same event differently;
- work out what triggered an event to take place in the short term or the long term.

What was Britain like in 1485?

_____ MISSION OBJECTIVES _____

• To work out what England was like in 1485 and its relationship with the neighbouring countries.

This book is about the people and events of Britain between 1485 and 1750, a time of great change. For you to see how important these changes were, you must first find out about Britain in 1485. Then, towards the end of this book, you will be asked to compare the Britain of 1485 with the Britain of 1750.

A lord

I am Henry VII, King of England. I rule other countries too. I won my crown on the battlefield and I intend to keep it. There are many rich and powerful men in this country, so I must work hard to control them.

Henry VII

We lords are rich and powerful... and the King knows it! We own lots of land and sometimes help the King to make decisions. If all lords joined together we could be strong enough to defeat the King.

England and Scotland are separate countries. The English and the Scots have fought a lot over the years. I think of the English as the 'old enemy' and truly hate them! There are about half a million Scots.

A Scotsman

Like most of the **population**, we are poor and live in the countryside. Some of the land is used for growing crops or grazing sheep, but most is woodland or wasteland. We live on what we grow. If we grow more than we need, we sell it at the local market in the nearest town. Most towns are still quite small but a few are growing fast. Only 10% of people live in the towns. There are about 2 million people who live in England now.

A Welsh prince

Over the years, English kings have tried to control us but have failed. They have only managed to control a small part of this country. About 800 000 people live here.

An Irish chief

The English control most of Wales but some areas are still run by **independent** Welsh princes like me. There are only about 200 000 people in Wales.

There is only one religion – Christianity. The Head of the Church is the Pope, who lives in Rome. Religion is a very important part of people's lives.

A priest

A villager

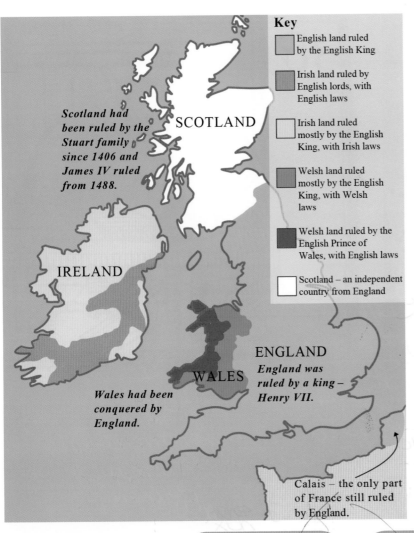

Key

English land ruled by the English King

Irish land ruled by English lords, with English laws

Irish land ruled mostly by the English King, with Irish laws

Welsh land ruled mostly by the English King, with Welsh laws

Welsh land ruled by the English Prince of Wales, with English laws

Scotland – an independent country from England

SCOTLAND

Scotland had been ruled by the Stuart family since 1406 and James IV ruled from 1488.

IRELAND

WALES

ENGLAND

England was ruled by a king – Henry VII.

Wales had been conquered by England.

Calais – the only part of France still ruled by England.

WISE-UP Words

independent
population

↵ **SOURCE A:** *Britain in 1485. England's king, Henry VII was known as King of England, Lord of Ireland and Prince of Wales. He ruled over England and had some powers in Ireland and Wales, but none in Scotland.*

SOURCE B: *Fifteenth-century Britain.* ↴

KING AND PARLIAMENT
England and Scotland had their own kings.

THE KNOWN WORLD
North America, South America, Australia and New Zealand were undiscovered by Europeans.

FOOD AND DRINK
British citizens had a basic diet.

CLOTHING
Clothing was a sign of status, as it is today. Only the very wealthy wore expensive fabrics.

HOMES
The rich lived in strong defensive homes, the poor lived in small, thatched-roofed cottages.

Britain in 1485

TRANSPORT
The rich on horseback; the poor walked! Roads were very poor.

COMMUNICATION
Mainly word of mouth.

RELIGION:
One common religion – Christianity. The Pope in Rome was the Head of the Christian Church – the Catholic Church that is!

FURNITURE
Solid and wooden, few chairs.

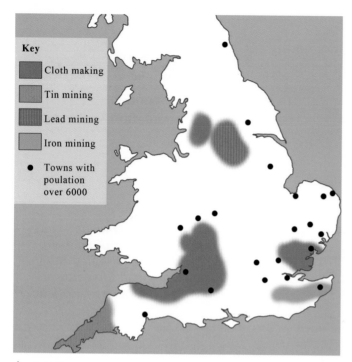

Key
- Cloth making
- Tin mining
- Lead mining
- Iron mining
- ● Towns with poulation over 6000

SOURCE C: *Common industries in Britain in 1485. As you can see, cloth making was England's most important industry and nearly every town would have had a group of spinners, weavers and dyers.*

SOURCE D: *A weaver.*

SOURCE E: *A fete at Bermondsey, near London around 1500, showing townspeople of all classes of society. Note the skyline in the background.*

! FACT Old Macdonald had a farm
There were about 8 million sheep in Britain in 1485 and only about 3 million people! The sheep were kept mainly to supply the cloth industry.

'There are old men living in my village who have noticed three things to be greatly changed. One is the many chimneys recently erected. The second is the beds. Their fathers used to sleep on straw on rough mats covered only with a sheet and a good round log under their heads. Pillows were only for women in childbed. The third is the change from wooden plates and spoons to silver or tin.'

↰ **SOURCE F:** *Written by William Harrison who lived in Essex in the 1500s.*

! FACT Money, money, money

The currency was pounds, shillings and pence. The '£' (a fancy L) was used for pound (from the Latin *'Libra'*) meaning a pound in weight, the 's' was used for shilling (an ancient English value) and 'd' was used for penny (from the Latin *'denarius'*) The penny was the basic unit of currency. Twelve pennies made a shilling and 20 shillings made a pound, so there were 240 pennies to the pound.

In the early 1500s, a farm worker could make a shilling a day – and bread (the main food) cost half a penny per loaf.

✚ Hungry for MORE

What was your town like in 1485? Can you find out anything about it? Try your local library, the Internet or ask your teacher.

Work

1 Write out the paragraph below, choosing one answer from each pair of brackets.

In 1485, the King of England was (Henry VII/Henry VIII). He also controlled most of (Wales/Scotland) and part of Ireland. (Wales/Scotland) was an independent country. Some land was used for (fishing/farming) but most of it was wasteland or (woodland/Disneyland). Nine out of (ten/nine) people lived in the (towns/countryside) and grew enough food to live on. If they grew (more/less) than they needed, they might go and sell it at the local (supermarket/market).

2 a Draw a bar chart to show the population of England, Scotland, Ireland and Wales in 1485. Your teacher will help you to set this out properly. Make sure you add a title.

   b Find out the population of England, Scotland, Ireland and Wales today. Draw another bar chart using these figures. Underneath it write a paragraph comparing the two bar charts.

   – Does England still have the largest population?

   – What is the second most populated country?

3 Look at Source E. What can you tell about life in the 1500s from this painting?

4 Look at Source F. According to the old men living in William Harrison's village in the 1500s, what are the three things that have changed most in recent times?

5 Divide a page into two columns. Write 'Britain in 1485' at the top of one column and 'Britain now' at the top of the other. List all the ways that Britain in 1485 was different from Britain today. Choose what you think are the three most important differences and write a sentence or two explaining why you made your choices.

___MISSION ACCOMPLISHED?___

• Can you recall five facts about England in 1485?

Was King Henry VII a gangster?

• To understand what problems Henry VII had to deal with when he became King of England and how he dealt with each of these issues.

Ever heard the word 'gangster'? There will certainly be some of you reading this who know what sort of person a gangster is. Before continuing with your studies on Henry VII, make sure you know what a gangster is.

For 30 years, in the fifteenth century, the York family and the Lancaster family had been fighting for control of England. By 1485, it was the Yorks who ruled the land. The most senior Yorkist, Richard, had been crowned King Richard III of England in 1483.

In August 1485, a member of the Lancaster family, Henry Tudor, decided to try to win the crown for his family. On 22 August, in a field near Bosworth, Leicestershire, the two armies fought each other.

King Richard decided to wear his crown into battle but this made him very easy to spot. As he charged towards his enemy, he was pulled from his horse by some of Henry's bodyguards. They cut Richard to pieces. Legend has it that they found Richard's bloodstained crown in a thorn bush before placing it on Henry Tudor's head. He became King Henry VII, the first Tudor king. The new king had won his crown by fighting. Now he had the job of keeping it.

The new king had major problems:

• The York family would probably seek revenge for the death of Richard III. Could he buy them off instead?

• Some of the country's landowning barons were very powerful and wealthy. They also kept their own private armies. How could he reduce their power?

• Kings need money for weapons, armies, large country houses and entertainment. Henry didn't have much. How could he get rich quick?

As you will see, King Henry would need to use every gangster trick in the book.

! FACT Cheeky monkey
Henry VII owned a pet monkey, which used to cause mayhem in his palaces. It once managed to open a box in which the King kept all his diaries... and ate them.

SOURCE D: *A painting of Henry VII dating from 1505. He sent his picture to a possible new wife after his first wife, Elizabeth of York, died in 1503. Notice he is clutching a rose in his right hand, one of the many Tudor symbols. We still use the rose today as an English symbol. Can you think where it is used?* ↱

Work

1 What is meant by the term 'gangster'?

2 Imagine you are Henry VII and have just been crowned King of England. Write a letter to one of your friends outlining your concerns as the new king. Think about the problems he faced as the new king.

So how did Henry solve his problems?

Henry spent a fortune on entertainment, lavish banquets, processions, tournaments, dancing and music. He once paid £30 (a huge amount) to a girl who danced for him. He even made his dogs wear fancy silk costumes! Even so, by the time of his death in 1509, Henry VII had left his surviving son, Henry, a fortune. England was at peace and his throne was safe.

 He married a woman from the House of York.

Henry settled the old argument between the Lancasters and the Yorks. In early 1486, he married Elizabeth of York, daughter of Edward VI. Now the Lancasters had a king and the Yorks had a queen.

The white rose symbol of the Yorks was added to the red rose symbol of the Lancaster family to make the Tudor Rose.

 He banned private armies.

Some barons paid their servants to act as an army for them. Henry banned this. He was worried a baron could use his own private army against the King. Henry once visited his friend, the Earl of Oxford, who had lined up his servants in uniform along his drive to welcome the King. Henry took a few moments to admire the beautiful uniforms... and then fined the earl £10 000 for keeping a private army!

 Henry made sure that he had the best cannons.

The cannon and gunpowder were changing warfare at this time. With some of the finest cannons in the land, Henry made the barons' castles unsafe.

 He made deals with other countries.

Henry had to raise taxes to pay for war with France, but then he managed to get the French King to pay him £150 000 not to fight. To make sure that England didn't get involved in a costly war with Spain, he got his eldest son, Arthur, married to a Spanish princess, Catherine of Aragon. When Arthur died, Henry got his younger son, also called Henry, married to her as well. He also got his daughter to marry the son of the King of Scotland.

 He made sure everyone knew he was king.

Henry wanted to be seen as a great king. He used family symbols to show people the strength of the Tudors. They appeared all over England in churches, cathedrals, palaces and manor houses.

The Tudor Rose.

The Beaufort Portcullis, the symbol of his mother Margaret.

Crown and thorn bush. Why do you think this symbol was used?

French lilies. Henry had spent a lot of time in France.

WISE-UP Words

gangster
symbols

4 He forced people to give him money.

Henry sent his ministers around England looking for sources of income. If they found a large manor house, they would force the owner to give them money. The ministers would argue that the house was so nice, the owner obviously had enough money to lend some to the King. Alternatively, if they came across a smaller house that was in need of repair, the ministers would still demand money. They would argue that the owner was obviously saving his money rather than spending it, and so must have enough savings to give some money to the King. The lenders would never get their money back.

1492
8 Jan: For the King to play at cards £5.00
16 Jan: For one who brought the King a lion £2.661/2
29 Jan: To Lady York for minstrels £1.00
12 Feb: For a fool who entertained 33p
29 April: For a flute player 33p
4 Jun: For the King's loss at gambling with his crossbow ... 66p
10 Jun: For a Spanish man who played the fool £2.00
30 Jun: For the King, which he lost at cards £40.00
31 Jul: For a horse and saddle to give to the Spanish fool . 921/2p
1 Aug: For children who sang in the garden 161/2p
1493
23 Jun: For making a bonfire on Midsummer Eve 50p
25 Aug: For a young girl who danced £30.00
24 Sept: For a man who had his bull baited 50p
1494
13 Jun: For a Spanish tennis player £2.00
14 Aug: For the King's loss at tennis £1.38

↳ **SOURCE B:** *Some payments made by Henry between 1492 and 1494, taken from court records.*

'Henry VII likes to be spoken about and looked up to by the whole world. In this he fails because he is not a great man. Although he claims many virtues, his love of money is too great!'

↳ **SOURCE C:** *Written by a Spanish visitor in a letter home in 1489.*

'In politics no one was as wise as him. He had a very good memory, a quick and alert mind, and always gave fair and short reasons ... Many were the languages he spoke. He was friendly. He had a clear skin and blue eyes. With all Christian princes he made alliances. His might was feared everywhere, both inside and outside his kingdom.

By the people he was obeyed as much as any other king. For many a day his land lived in piece and quiet. In battle his successes against his enemies was almost miraculous. During danger he calculated in a cold and clever way. He got wind of any treason plotted against him. Immense were his treasures and riches, and fair his buildings in the latest style.'

↳ **SOURCE D:** *Spoken by the preacher at Henry's funeral in 1509.*

Work

1 Read Source B.

  a Name five different amusements that Henry enjoyed.

  b Look carefully. What evidence is there, other than the £2 paid to him, that Henry enjoyed watching the Spanish fool?

2 Again, imagine you are Henry VII and you have been on the throne a number of years. Write back to your friend and tell them how you have dealt with the problems that faced you.
  – Have you made friends with the York family? If so, how?
  – Do you feel secure from enemies, both inside England and abroad?
  – Are you rich? If so, how did you make your money? What sort of lifestyle do you lead?

3 Look back at your definition of a 'gangster'. Was Henry VII like a gangster?

MISSION ACCOMPLISHED?

• Can you list three problems that Henry VII faced when he became King of England and can you list three ways that he dealt with them?

HOW RELIGIOUS WERE THE TUDOR MONARCHS?

In medieval England, almost everybody was a Catholic and followed the instructions of the Pope in Rome. All of that changed under the Tudors. Religion in England was never the same as one Tudor after another changed the way God was worshipped in England. These dramatic changes didn't just affect the kings and queens, but ordinary people all over the country. This meant that your religion could place you in a powerful position one minute and in danger of a horrible death the next! Thousands of people died or saw their lives ruined as different rulers forced one change after another. So what were these changes? Why did they make them? And just how religious were the Tudor monarchs?

1: What was young Henry VIII like?

———— MISSION OBJECTIVES ————
- To understand how young Henry VIII spent his time and money.
- To decide whether Henry was religious when he was a young man.

Everybody has heard of Henry VIII. Most people think they know a few things about him too. They usually say:
- He was a big fat bloke.
- He had six wives… or was it eight?
- He beheaded most of his wives.

Some of these statements are true. Henry did have six wives but he didn't chop the heads off most of them; although he did get someone to behead two! As for him being a big fat bloke – well yes he was – but only for the last few years of his life. In fact, on his forty-fifth birthday, Henry was the same size as he was when he was 23 – and at that age, Henry was a fine sportsman. As a young man, he enjoyed hunting, tennis, wrestling, archery and jousting. He was even known to enjoy a good snowball fight in winter. Henry wrote music and poetry and could speak four languages. So despite having a bit of a weight problem when he was older, Henry was an impressive man when he was crowned in 1509.

As you will learn, many fantastic facts surround the life of Henry VIII. In fact, Henry was desperate to become known as a super king and even liked to call himself 'Henry the Great'. But although he is most famous for his wives, the most important events in Henry's life were the religious changes he made. Not only did they affect religion in Henry's time, they changed religion in England and Wales for good.

SOURCE A: *A portrait of Henry VIII showing him in his late twenties.* ↱

TONIGHT ONLY

AT HAMPTON COURT PALACE
IN THE PRESENCE OF
HENRY THE GREAT

A ROYAL GALA PERFORMANCE

A feast fit for a king – beef, pork, lamb, chicken, eggs, venison, pigeon pie, rabbit, wine and apple tart

Anne Penn – plays the harp
Fat Scotty the jester – jokes and rude stories
Matthew Morrish – the little juggling stilt walker
The fighting Dunkley Brothers – will wrestle each other and any challengers – Prizes to be won
Dance the Pavane, the Volta and the Galliard to the wonderful music makers followed by – STOP PRESS – Hear our king's latest song, 'GREENSLEEVES'

Henry was a very religious man and, like most people in the country at the time, he was Catholic. He visited church at least three times a day and even wrote a book supporting the Pope, who was the Head of the Catholic Church. Henry was such a good Catholic that in 1521, the Pope rewarded Henry with the title 'Fidei Defensor', which means 'Defender of the Faith'. Henry liked the title so much that he made sure the letters FD were on all the coins made in his name. You can still see the letters FD or the words 'Fid. Def.' on some British coins today – have a look yourself.

However, by 1533, Henry had fallen out with the Pope, who **excommunicated** him, meaning he was expelled from the Catholic Church. This was a very serious punishment at the time because it meant that the person could not talk to a priest about their sins. If a priest did not forgive you for your sins, then you wouldn't get to heaven. So how did Henry VIII and the Pope fall out with each other? What had Henry done that was so terrible that he received the worst kind of religious punishment? The next few pages chart an amazing story.

Henry the big spender

Henry loved to bet on anything – cards, dice, tennis, wrestling, or jousting. He used to win (and lose) the equivalent of thousands of pounds every day. Henry also loved to dress in the smartest, most expensive clothes. His silk shirts, gold buttons and jewel-encrusted jackets would have cost a fortune. So, too, would his legendary parties, held at any of Henry's 55 palaces.

WISE-UP Words

Catholic
excommunicated
Pope

! FACT Henry, the good Catholic
Henry's book said how good the Catholic Church was. In it, he wrote that the Pope, as Head of the Catholic Church, did a good job. Henry even wrote about marriage, which he said should be forever – one woman, for life.

Work

Your task is to write a profile of the young King Henry VIII.

Search through the text to find out details about the young king, using the following subheadings to guide your writing:

- Henry the athlete
- Henry the good Catholic
- Henry the big spender.

Finally, write your own opinion in answer to the following question – Should the young King Henry have been called 'Henry the Great'?

! FACT What a job
Henry VIII employed someone to wipe his bottom! He was officially called the 'Groom of the Stool'. It was a much prized job because the employee got to spend so much time with the King!

——— **MISSION ACCOMPLISHED?** ———

- Could you name a sport that Henry enjoyed?
- Could you tell somebody about a strange thing that Henry spent his money on?
- Do you know why the Pope called him 'Defender of the Faith' and have you decided if he deserved it?

Henry's problems with religion started with his love life. His first wife was a Spanish princess called Catherine of Aragon. He first met her when she came to England to marry his big brother Arthur! So how did Henry end up marrying her? What problems did this cause? And what did his relationship with Catherine mean for the future of religion in England?

2: Henry VIII, Rome and divorce

MISSION OBJECTIVES

- To understand how and why Henry VIII fell out with the Pope.
- To know how this affected the life of Henry and religion in the whole of England.

A marriage between Prince Arthur and Princess Catherine would mean friendship between England and Spain. However, Arthur died only a year after the marriage. To avoid sending widow Catherine home to Spain and upsetting her father, Henry VII arranged for his second son, Henry, to marry her. The wedding took place in 1509, the same year that the old King Henry VII died. Seventeen-year-old Henry became King Henry VIII and Catherine of Aragon was his first queen.

Henry and Catherine were a popular and loving couple. In 1513, whilst Henry was in France, Catherine ran the country for him. Her army even beat a Scottish army at the Battle of Flodden. Catherine brought Henry a present home from the battle… the dead King of Scotland's coat, still stained with his blood.

Henry and Catherine were happily married for nearly 20 years. Henry once said, 'If I were still free, I would choose her for a wife above all others.' What a romantic man! But the marriage didn't last. As we all know, he had five more wives after Catherine… so what went wrong?

Henry desperately wanted a son.

Catherine gives birth to six children, but only one, a girl called Mary, survives.

By 1527, Henry thinks Catherine is too old to have any more children.

Henry wants to divorce Catherine. He'd fallen in love with another woman too – Anne Boleyn!

Henry gets his lawyers to secretly look into whether his marriage to Catherine is legal or not.

The marriage was found to be legal – but Henry still wanted his divorce.

In 1533, Henry gave himself the divorce he desired.

Henry ignored the Pope. He made himself Head of the Church of England instead of the Pope.

The Pope was furious but Henry could do as he pleased.

Henry could now marry Anne Boleyn.

Henry married his second wife, Anne Boleyn, in the summer of 1533. She was already pregnant.

Anne gave birth to a girl, Elizabeth, in September 1533. Henry was very disappointed – why?

Henry's desire for a baby boy began a series of events that altered religion in England forever. In one move, he had his divorce and made himself more powerful. The Pope in Rome no longer had the English Church under his control – Henry did and all its wealth too! To this day, the Head of the Church of England is the king or queen. Yet despite this change of church leader and the closing of the monasteries, Henry only really made one other major religious change. From 1538, he ordered that in every church the Bible was to be read in English, not Latin. At last, ordinary people could understand what their religion was teaching them.

Henry's only chance of a divorce was to ask the Pope. He was the only man who could give Henry what he wanted.

Henry hated the fact that the Pope had this power over him… but he had a plan.

! FACT

New titles for new things

Historians like to give titles to anything different! Henry's changes to the Church are known as the '**Reformation**' because Henry was reforming (another word for 'changing') the English Church.

When he closed down the monasteries, it was known as the '**Dissolution**' of the monasteries. Dissolution is another word for 'breaking up'.

Some of the monks in England didn't support Henry's new Church of England. They supported the Pope.

So he closed down all the monasteries and the land was sold.

The monasteries were very wealthy and the King made a good profit.

But the Pope was furious again. Not only had Henry ignored him and closed all of the Catholic monasteries in England, but he had now stolen all their treasures.

★ WISE-UP Words

dissolution
reformation

Work ⌐◠◠◠.

1 The following dates are important ones from Henry's marriage to his first wife:

1533 • 1527 • 1513 • 1501 • 1509

Write each date, in chronological order, on a separate line. Beside each date, write what happened in that year. Be careful – LOTS happens in one of the years!

2 What do we see as unusual today about Henry's marriage to Catherine of Aragon?

3 Which of the following statements do you think was most important in making Henry want a divorce from Catherine of Aragon?
  • Henry was bored with Catherine.
  • Henry's desire to have a son.
  • Henry's love of Anne Boleyn.
  • Henry disagreed with the Pope over religion.

Give reasons for your answer.

4 a Why did Henry want a son?

  b What do you think about his reason?

5 Why did Henry close down the monasteries? Give more than one reason.

6 Write a sentence or two to explain the following words:

reformation • dissolution

—— MISSION ACCOMPLISHED? ——

• Have you decided why Henry wanted a divorce?
• Do you know why this made him fall out with the Pope?
• Can you name two ways in which Henry changed religion in England?

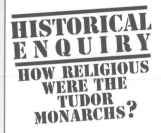

HISTORICAL ENQUIRY
HOW RELIGIOUS WERE THE TUDOR MONARCHS?

Today, only a small minority of people visit church on a regular basis. In fact, according to one survey, more people go shopping on Sundays than go to a Church service. Things were very different in Tudor times. In a world without televisions, cinemas or shopping centres, the Church was the centre of most people's lives. It provided a welcome meeting place, somewhere to enjoy summer fairs and, of course, to worship God. Everybody in Tudor England believed in God but for the first time people started to question how the Church was run. People took religion very seriously and this doubting of what they saw as the word of God led to a great deal of upheaval and many thousands of deaths. So why were some people becoming unhappy with the Church? What did they believe instead? And what did this mean for religion in Europe?

3: What did Protestants protest about?

MISSION OBJECTIVES

- To understand why some people became unhappy with the Catholic Church.
- To know how Protestants got their name and what they believed.

Spreading the word

People in Tudor times used God to explain things they didn't understand. Nasty illnesses or infections were seen as punishment from God. If the harvest was bad, it was because God wished it so. They also believed that heaven and hell were real places. If you led a good life on earth and prayed regularly, then you would probably go to heaven when you died. However, if you were a bad person who committed crimes and didn't attend church regularly, then you would definitely end up in hell.

By 1500, there were thousands of books available to read on many topics. There were lots of books on religion and even copies of the Bible were available in English rather than Latin. For the first time, ordinary men and women could read it for themselves instead of having to go to church and listen to what the priest told them. Some people who were not priests started to think very deeply about the Church and wonder whether everything they had ever been told was entirely correct.

In 1517, a German monk called Martin Luther wrote out a long list of criticisms of the Catholic Church and nailed it to his local church door. Luther wanted the Catholic Church to change and soon his ideas and beliefs attracted many followers. By 1529, the followers were known as **Protestants** because they *protested* against the Catholic Church. Now there were two religious groups in Europe who believed in a Christian version of God – the Catholics and the Protestants. However, both wanted to worship Him in slightly different ways.

CRITICISM NO. 1
The Church was too rich!
- The Church owned about one-third of all the land in England. An ordinary peasant had to give 10% of their harvest (a tithe) to the priest every year. Some felt that the bishops, priests and monks lived in luxury, whilst the poor suffered.

CRITICISM NO. 2
The priests didn't lead a very 'holy' life.
Some priests had a few jobs and neglected their work. Villagers once told the Bishop of Hereford:
'The priest puts his horses and sheep in the churchyard… he was away for six weeks and made no arrangements for a substitute. Sir John (the priest) spends his time in the taverns and there his tongue is loosened to the scandal of everyone. He is living with a woman, Margaret, and he cannot read nor write and so cannot look after the parishioners' souls.'
Ordinary people did not think some priests were setting a very good example to the people in the village or town.

CRITICISM NO. 3
Ordinary people couldn't understand the church services.
The Bible was written in Latin and the church services were held in this language as well. People said they found it difficult to feel close to God if they couldn't understand what was being said in church.

SOURCE A: *A print of the execution of William Tyndale. He was executed for translating the Bible into English so that ordinary people could read it.*

SOURCE B: *Martin Luther's protest against the Pope changed religion forever.*

WISE-UP Words

indulgences
purgatory
Protestants
tithe

! FACT Rival religions

The **Catholic** way to worship:
- The Pope is Head of the Catholic Church and is chosen by God.
- The Bible and prayer books are written in Latin.
- A church should be a bright and colourful place to worship God, with pictures on the walls, stained-glass windows, a large stone altar, silver cups and crosses, and priests in magnificent robes.

The **Protestant** way to worship:
- A country's monarch should be the Head of the Church.
- The Bible and prayer books should be in a language that the worshippers understand – not in Latin.
- A church should be a plain and simple place to worship God. Money shouldn't be wasted on decorations or robes for the priest.

Work

1 In your own words, explain why religion and the Church played such an important part in people's lives.

2 Explain the origin of the word 'Protestant'.

3 The year is 1517. Imagine you are Martin Luther, angry with the Catholic Church. Using the information on these pages to help you, write your own list of criticisms of the Church. You could try and make your work look old – ask your teacher for advice on how to do this.

CRITICISM NO. 4

Poor people couldn't afford 'indulgences'.

When a person died, they went to heaven or hell. It was thought you passed through a place called **purgatory** on the way. In purgatory, people believed you were punished for any sins you may have committed whilst you were alive. It wasn't meant to be a nice place to stay for very long. When you were alive, you could buy 'indulgences' from a bishop. This meant that you travelled through purgatory quicker. Rich people could buy lots of indulgences. Poor people didn't think it was fair. They thought that they were being punished for being poor.

MISSION ACCOMPLISHED?

- Can you name three things about the Catholic Church in Tudor times that made some people unhappy?
- Do you know two differences between the Catholic and Protestant ways to worship God?
- Could you explain to somebody what the word 'Protestant' means?

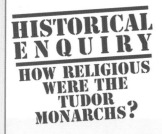
Henry VIII had more wives than any other English king. Being his wife must have been a very tricky business. They may have enjoyed a luxury lifestyle, but there were enormous risks involved. So which wife did he accuse of being a witch? Who did he divorce for being too ugly? And who did he have executed for having a boyfriend before she met him?

4: Who'd want to marry Henry VIII?

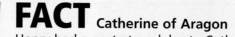

MISSION OBJECTIVES

- To understand why Henry married so many women.
- To know what happened to each of his wives.
- To be able to advise his sixth wife on how to survive being married to Henry.

Your task is to look through the tangled love life of Henry. Imagine that you are a friend of Catherine Parr. She is a sensible, intelligent and kind 31-year-old widow and 52-year-old King Henry wants to marry her. She would be Henry's sixth wife. Despite her family's pleasure that the King has chosen her, she is a little bit worried, perhaps frightened. The marriage has been organised and the date set for 12 July 1543. Your job, as her friend, is to give her advice. Carefully read about each of Henry's previous wives and what went wrong for them. Catherine is looking to you for guidance. How might she be able to keep the King happy? What shouldn't she do?

Let's start by looking at the ageing king…

- 52 years old.
- Cruel, bad tempered and paranoid – once he was so convinced that someone would try to kill him as he slept that he instructed a bricklayer to brick him into his bedroom at night.
- So fat that he had to be put onto his horse with a hoist.
- He complained about headaches, fever, smallpox and malaria. His legs were covered with ulcers, which later turned to gangrene. One visitor wrote that Henry 'had the worst legs in the world'.

CATHERINE OF ARAGON: Wife Number 1: 1509–33

- Catholic.
- A Spanish princess, once married to Henry's older brother. She brought friendship with Spain.
- Clever and popular.
- All her male babies died but she had a daughter called Mary who survived.
- Henry thought Catherine was old and boring when she reached 40 years of age. He divorced her.

! FACT Catherine of Aragon

Henry had a party to celebrate Catherine's death in 1536 (there were rumours at the time that she'd been poisoned). He even wore yellow clothes, the traditional colour of celebration!

ANNE BOLEYN: Wife Number 2: 1533–36

- Protestant.
- Young, sexy and very fashionable.
- At first, made Henry wait for sex until he married her.
- Had a daughter, Elizabeth. Henry sulked for weeks because he wanted a boy.
- Miscarried a baby boy in 1536.
- Henry accused Anne of having sex with four men and her brother (yes, her brother). Despite no proof, she was beheaded in 1536.

! FACT Ann Boleyn

Anne was born with an extra finger on one hand. People said that this was a sign that she was a witch. Anne made enemies easily.

JANE SEYMOUR: Wife Number 3: 1536–37

- Protestant.
- Calm, gentle and caring. She tried hard to be friends with Henry's daughters.
- Made Henry wait for sex until he married her.
- Had a son, Edward. Henry was delighted – a boy at last!
- Jane died of an infection a few days after the birth.

ANNE OF CLEVES: Wife Number 4: 1540

- Protestant.
- Cleves was an area of what is now Germany, close to Flanders and France. Henry married Anne because it brought friendship between England, Wales and this powerful European region.
- She was serious and unfashionable. Friends tried to teach her some of Henry's favourite card games but she didn't understand them.
- Henry had seen a painting of her and liked what he saw. However, when he saw her for real, he described her as a 'fat mare [horse] from Flanders'.
- Henry divorced her.

! FACT Jayne Seymour

Henry really loved Jane. More than two years went by before he married again, the longest gap between his marriages. When he died, he was buried next to her.

CATHERINE HOWARD: Wife Number 5: 1540–42

- Protestant.
- Young, lively and very pretty.
- She flirted with lots of men… and Henry found out. She once finished off a letter to her lover with the words, 'Yours as long as life endures'. Henry was furious.
- Henry also found out that she had several serious boyfriends before she met the King. A queen should not have a past like this!
- She was executed.

! FACT Anne of Cleves

Henry's six-month marriage to Anne was never consummated (they never had sex). After the divorce, Anne was given land, money and the rather strange official title of the 'King's sister'.

Work

Now write Catherine a letter giving her advice about her forthcoming marriage. In your letter include:

– Details of his previous five marriages:
- What attracted Henry to each of them?
- What went wrong with each marriage?
- What happened to each of them?

– Top tips on how to keep Henry happy and interested in her. Remember how old he is and what sort of wife he needs now.

! FACT Catherine Howard

When Catherine found out she was going to be beheaded, she ran shouting and screaming towards Henry to beg his forgiveness. He locked the door and ignored her. Her crying ghost is still said to haunt the same corridor at Hampton Court Palace.

✚ Hungry for MORE

What happened to Catherine Parr? Find out about her life with Henry… and after.

——— MISSION ACCOMPLISHED? ———

- Can you explain what went wrong with Henry's first five marriages?
- Have you advised Catherine Parr on how best to survive married life?

Despite six marriages, Henry VIII left only three children behind when he died on 28 January 1547. Edward was nine, Elizabeth was 14 and Mary was a woman of 31. Henry had absolutely no doubt as to who he would leave in control of the country – the nine year old of course! The young prince may have been the same age as a Year Five student – but he was male! Henry, and most other men in Tudor England, believed this made him a much better choice as ruler than his older sisters. So what kind of king was young Edward? Which religion did he follow? And what did this mean for the way people worshipped God in England?

5: Edward VI: the boy king

MISSION OBJECTIVES

- To be able to explain how and why Henry's son changed religion in England.
- To decide what kind of boy Edward VI was.

SOURCE A: *Inside a Catholic church.*

Rood screen (to separate priest from worshippers)

Pictures to explain Bible stories

Sanctuary lamps

Stained glass

Statue of the Virgin Mary

Gold crosses, candlesticks and chalices

Expensive robes

Stone alter

Changes in religion

As you have learned, Henry VIII had made some important changes to religion. He had closed all the monasteries (and taken their money), allowed the Bible to be read in English (not Latin) and most importantly, made himself, and future kings and queens, Head of the Church of England (instead of the Pope). Henry didn't make any more major changes to religion and most people, including the King, still thought of themselves as Catholic. However, Henry's son Edward believed deeply in the Protestant faith. As a Protestant, he thought that the Catholic Church made people worship God in the wrong way. He felt that God should be worshipped in a plain

and simple manner. As he was Head of the Church, he could alter it in any way he wished. Once again, religion in England was about to change!

Many people, especially in the countryside, didn't like all the changes to the way they worshipped. They loved the old services and churches, and in some areas there were rebellions. The leaders of one rebellion in Cornwall saw just how ruthless young King Edward could be… he sent in his soldiers to hang the rebels from the nearest trees.

Edward had always been a sickly child and constantly in need of a doctor's attention. He used to have his bedroom

Hungry for MORE

Close to his death, Edward named his 16-year-old cousin, Lady Jane Grey, as next in line to the throne. She later became known as the 'Nine days queen'.
• Who was she?
• Why did Edward choose her?
• How did she get her nickname?
• What happened to her?

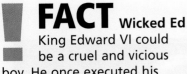

FACT Wicked Ed

King Edward VI could be a cruel and vicious boy. He once executed his uncle for accidentally killing his favourite pet.

↵ SOURCE B: *A painting of Edward VI, painted in about 1550.*

Royal coat of arms

Prayer book in English, not Latin

Wall plaques with Lord's prayer and parts of the Bible in English

Stained glass smashed, replaced with plain glass

Pulpit for preaching the new English services

Plain clothes. Priests could get married too.

Simple wooden table

Rood screen removed

↳ SOURCE C: *New Protestant ways.*

walls washed down three times a day to keep him free from disease. But by the age of 15, he was dying of a lung disease called **tuberculosis**. His hair fell out, his nails came off and his fingers and toes began to loosen and drop away at the joints. Edward died on 6 July 1553. He had no children, so his older sister, Mary, became the new queen. She was a deeply religious Catholic. Protestant England was about to change.

WISE-UP Words

obituary
tuberculosis

Work

1 Why do you think Edward became king after his father's death and not Mary or Elizabeth?

2 a Describe what you would have seen if you had entered a Catholic church before 1547.

b Now imagine you visited the same church after Edward had made his Protestant changes and describe what you see.

3 Design and write an obituary for King Edward VI – an **obituary** briefly tells of some of the most important events, achievements and the personality of the person who recently died. Begin with Edward's birth on 12 October 1537 and end with his death on 6 July 1553 at the age of just 15.

MISSION ACCOMPLISHED?

• Do you know which religion Edward VI followed?
• Can you name three changes Edward made to churches or church services in England?
• Could you tell somebody what Edward's personality was like and what happened to him?

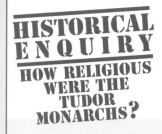

Nicknames are sometimes used between friends who know each other very well. Other times, they are used by people to be nasty. Mary I had a very nasty nickname: Bloody Mary. Why? What could she have done to be remembered in such a horrible way? And did she deserve it?

6: How bloody was 'Bloody Mary'?

———————————— MISSION OBJECTIVES ————————————
- To understand how and why 'Bloody Mary' got her nickname.
- To decide whether she deserved her nasty nickname.

Mary I

When she became queen in 1553, Mary was unmarried, 37 years old and a devout Catholic. Some people were delighted to have Mary as Queen. They didn't like all the religious changes that had taken place in Edward's reign. They looked forward to a time when Mary would bring back the old Catholic ways.

Mary married the Catholic King Philip of Spain but this was seen as a bad move. Philip and the Spanish were very unpopular in England. Would this Spanish King interfere in the running of the country?

As soon as she was crowned, Mary started to undo all the changes her father and brother had made:

- England was officially a Catholic country once more.
- The Pope was the Head of the English and Welsh Churches again.
- The churches were redecorated – stone altars, bright painted walls, statues, gold crosses and candlesticks were added.
- Married priests were made to leave their wives.
- Church services and prayer books were in Latin once more.

Mary's changes didn't please the Protestants, who were becoming fed up of this religious see-saw. Her message to them was simple – change religion or be punished! You might now see how Mary acquired her nickname.

SOURCE A: *A painting of Bloody Mary.*

'All the people of London rejoiced and made many great fires. They set out tables and feasted. The bells rang till ten of the clock at night.'

SOURCE B: *From a letter written at the time, celebrating the arrival of the new queen.*

'I will spare the life of Lady Jane.'

SOURCE C: *Lady Jane Grey was named queen by the previous king, Edward VI. She didn't last long at all. Mary's troops marched into London and arrested her. Mary promised not to kill Jane but soon ordered the execution of her, her husband and other family members!*

'About 300 people were burned to death all over the country because they refused to worship the Catholic way. Most of these were humble shopkeepers, carpenters, farmers and housewives.'

SOURCE D: *From 'History Alive 1 1485–1714', by Peter Moss (1980).*

'Si corpus meum tradi igni, caritate non habeam, nihil utilitatis &c.
D. Smith'

Master Ridley. I will remember your suit.

In manus tuas domine, Ridley

Latimer. father of Heaven receive my soul.

⌐ SOURCE E: *The burning of Latimer and Ridley, two Protestants who refused to become Catholics.*

'There were burnt 5 bishops, 21 ministers, 8 gentlemen, 84 workers, 100 farmers, servants and labourers, 26 wives, 20 widows, 9 girls, 2 boys and 2 infants.'

⌐ SOURCE F: *From a book called 'Book of Martyrs' by John Fox, a Protestant. A **martyr** is someone who is prepared to die for what they believe.*

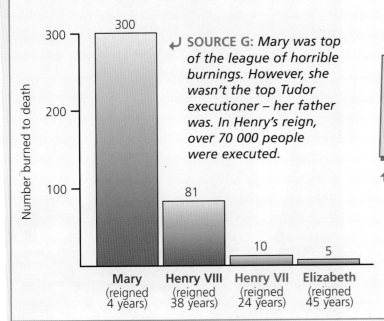

↵ SOURCE G: *Mary was top of the league of horrible burnings. However, she wasn't the top Tudor executioner – her father was. In Henry's reign, over 70 000 people were executed.*

Number burned to death

Mary (reigned 4 years)	Henry VIII (reigned 38 years)	Henry VII (reigned 24 years)	Elizabeth (reigned 45 years)
300	81	10	5

Work

1 a Divide your page into two columns: 'Bloody Mary' and 'Unlucky Mary'. Read through each source and decide if you think it suggests whether Mary deserved her nickname or not. If you think it does, write a brief description of the source in the 'Bloody Mary' column. If you think it doesn't, write a brief description of it in the 'Unlucky Mary' column.

b Overall, do you think Mary deserves her nasty nickname? Give reasons for your answer.

2 Sources B and H were written by the same person. How had public opinion about their queen changed during Mary's time as queen?

3 Read Source F.

a Why might you not be able to trust everything that is written in Fox's book?

b Do you think this book was published during Mary's reign? Give reasons for your answer.

'... when Mary died, all the churches of London did ring, and at night did make bonfires and set tables in the street and did eat and drink and be merry...'

⌐ SOURCE H: *From a letter written at the time of Mary's death.*

'Mary was a deeply religious woman and devoted to the same Catholic faith as her mother. All of the monarchs that have followed her have been Protestants so Mary's history has been written by Protestant historians. They have not been kind to her.'

⌐ SOURCE I: *An extract from a modern history book.*

MISSION ACCOMPLISHED?

- Could you tell someone two reasons why Mary may have earned her nasty nickname?
- Have you decided whether she deserved to be called 'Bloody Mary'?

You've all heard it. Most of you will have sung it. Mothers sing it to babies; children sing it in nursery classes and students sing it in the playground. It sounds like a nice, friendly rhyme about a girl called Mary. But would you sing it if you really knew what each line was about? The poem is about someone called Mary but she's not a little girl. The Mary in the rhyme is 'Bloody Mary', queen from 1553 to 1558 and famous for ordering the burning of over 300 Protestants. So what is the rhyme about? What do all those strange words mean? And who would have written such a thing?

7: A nasty nursery rhyme

MISSION OBJECTIVES

- To understand the hidden meaning of the popular nursery rhyme 'Mary, Mary, quite contrary'.
- To decide what religion the writer of the rhyme would have belonged to.

Read through the poem carefully and then look through the fact boxes on these pages. Try to match them with each line. Prepare to be astonished! After you have read these pages you might think twice about singing it again.

> Mary, Mary, quite contrary,
> How does your garden grow?
> With silver bells
> And cockleshells,
> And pretty maids all in a row.

! FACT Problems in childbirth
Mary was rumoured to have had some children, but each little girl was **stillborn** – Mary was supposed to have had them buried secretly in a long row of graves.

! FACT Pregnant... or not?
Mary longed for a baby. She was delighted when she thought she was pregnant soon after marrying her husband, King Philip of Spain. However, she soon found out that she wasn't pregnant at all; her stomach pains were in fact the symptoms of a terrible disease, possibly cancer. One line of the rhyme **ridicules** the fact that nothing will grow inside her.

! FACT A poor taste in music
Mary enjoyed listening to the sound of church bells. This music was unfashionable at the time.

SOURCE A:
A portrait of Mary and Philip. ↱

! FACT Changing her mind

'Contrary' means 'opposite'. If a person is contrary, it often means that they take a different view just for the sake of it. Mary was accused of being awkward by wanting to change England back to a Catholic country so soon after it had become a Protestant one.

! FACT King Philip of Spain – the love rat

Mary's husband wasn't very loving. King Philip hardly ever saw her during their marriage. Also, he had affairs with lots of other women. In Tudor England, this was called **cuckolding**. Which line do you think this is referring to?

WISE-UP Words

adulterous
cuckolding
ridicule   stillborn

Have you worked it out? Can you match the five fact boxes to the five lines of the poem? Can you see how cruel the rhyme is? It must have been made up by someone who really hated Mary. What you thought was a harmless nursery rhyme about a girl called Mary was really a hateful, spiteful rhyme about an awkward woman with an **adulterous** husband, stillbirth, and the desire for a child, based on gossip and hearsay.

+ Hungry for MORE

This isn't the only cruel or nasty nursery rhyme. 'Jack and Jill' doesn't have a very happy ending, 'Rock a bye baby' ends in disaster and as for poor old 'Humpty Dumpty'… And we sing all of these to little babies. Try to find out more about some famous nursery rhymes. 'Ring a Ring a Roses', 'Humpty Dumpty' and 'Little Jack Horner' all have fascinating stories surrounding them.

Work

1 a Copy out each line of the nursery rhyme but leave some space underneath each line.

  b Underneath each line, explain what it really means, in your own words.

2 Do you think the writer of the rhyme was a Protestant or a Catholic? Explain your answer.

3 This rhyme was once described as a 'lot of old, nasty gossip'. What do you think this means? Explain your answer carefully.

4 Imagine you are the person who wrote the poem. Try to justify why you wrote such a spiteful poem. Use what you have learned about Mary to help you.

—— **MISSION ACCOMPLISHED?** ——

• Could you explain to somebody what the nursery rhyme 'Mary, Mary, quite contrary' is really about?

• Have you decided what kind of person would write such a nasty rhyme and why?

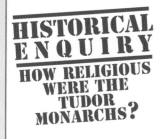
On 17 November 1558, Mary I died. Her marriage to Philip II of Spain had produced no children, so her half-sister Elizabeth became the new Queen of England. Elizabeth had spent much of her life as third in line for the throne and was lucky to have survived Mary's reign – her mother had taken Mary's mother's place as Henry's wife, after all! When Elizabeth heard of her half-sister's death, she fell to her knees and said, 'This is the Lord's doing and it is marvellous in our eyes.' So which religion did Elizabeth follow? What changes did she make? And what did her arrival on the throne mean for the way people worshipped God in England?

8: Elizabeth's middle way

MISSION OBJECTIVES

- To understand how Elizabeth tried to end the Tudor religious turmoil.
- To know which faith Elizabeth belonged to.
- To understand how this caused another Catholic clampdown.

The religious settlement

Elizabeth was going to return the country to the Protestant faith but had no intention of repeating the chaos caused by her half-brother and half-sister. Elizabeth was not a religious fanatic and wanted to avoid the extremes of both Protestants and Catholics. That way, she hoped she would please most English people and avoid a civil war.

A compromise with Catholics

Elizabeth made herself Governor, not Head, of the Church of England in order to please Catholics. This meant that Catholics – if they wanted to – could still think of the Pope as Head of the Church.

I'm the guv'nor!

Bishops were kept to please Catholics but services were in English to please Protestants.

Our Father...

Priests were allowed to marry to please the Protestants and a new Prayer Book replaced the one from Edward's reign that was so hated by Catholics.

The Catholic service was changed to please the Protestants but strict Catholics, who didn't want to attend the new services, weren't severely punished. They had to pay a fine for staying at home and became known recusants.

Did the 'middle way' work?

Although it pleased most people, **extremists** of both sides were left deeply unhappy by Elizabeth's **Religious Settlement**. Very strict Protestants, known as Puritans, didn't want to compromise with Catholics. They wanted to destroy the Pope and his whole religion. Devout Catholics believed that the Protestants were doing the work of the Devil and were damning the whole country to Hell. In fact, the Pope excommunicated Elizabeth and claimed that she was the daughter of a 'sorceress'! He then declared that anyone that killed her would be doing God's work and would guarantee their place in Heaven. This made it very difficult for Elizabeth to tolerate Catholics in England – as any one of them could be plotting her death! As a result, she decided to make life a little tougher for England's Catholics.

The Catholic clampdown

Elizabeth's spymaster, Sir Francis Walsingham, kept a close eye on all the major Catholics with informers and double agents. New laws were passed that meant that Catholic priests would now be tried and executed for treason. The fine that **recusants** had to pay was heavily increased in order to force them to leave the country but many were thrown in prison when they ran out of money. The prospect of being hung, drawn and quartered was not enough to stop many Catholic priests and they continued to hold their Catholic services in secret. Some were kept hidden in priest holes to avoid detection. But Elizabeth's long reign of 44 years meant that there was to be no Catholic comeback and the Protestant faith was firmly established in England. It remains an officially Protestant country to this day.

⬆ **SOURCE A:** *Catholic priests hid from Elizabeth's soldiers in secret 'priest holes' in manor houses.*

★ WISE-UP Words

extremists
recusants
Religious Settlement

! FACT Holy smoke!

The penalty for sheltering a Catholic priest was death but many Catholics saw it as their religious duty to keep their way of worship alive. Hiding places were built under stairs and behind false walls. Some priests hid up chimneys but Walsingham's men started lighting fires every time they searched a house. The soldiers would often stop in suspected houses for days, listening for the slightest noise that would betray a hidden priest.

Work ⌇

1 Explain what the word 'compromise' means.

2 Copy the following sentences into your books:
   – Elizabeth made herself Governor of the Church of England.
   – Bishops were allowed to stay in their jobs.
   – Priests were allowed to get married.
   – Edward VI's prayer book was replaced.
   – Recusants were allowed to miss Church services.

   After each sentence, write 'Catholic' if it was meant to keep Catholics happy and 'Protestant' if it was designed to please Protestants.

3 Did Elizabeth's 'middle way' work? Write a paragraph explaining your answer (you might want to mention the Pope!).

——— MISSION ACCOMPLISHED? ———

• Can you explain how Elizabeth tried to please both Catholics and Protestants?

• Do you know why Elizabeth decided to treat Catholics more harshly later in her reign? Could you tell somebody how Catholic priests tried to practice their religion in secret?

Leonardo – the man who wanted to know everything

MISSION OBJECTIVES

- To know who Leonardo da Vinci was and why he is such an important historical figure.
- To be able to explain what the Renaissance was.

One of the most important inventions in the history of mankind is the printing press. Before its invention in around 1450, all books had to be written out by hand – making books both very rare and very expensive. The ability to print pages meant books could be produced far quicker and much cheaper – meaning more and more people could afford them. This quickly turned reading – and writing – books into a craze that swept throughout Europe. Many people have compared the invention of the printing press to the invention of the Internet. Both allowed ideas and information to spread far more quickly than they had before. No longer did people have to ask the local priest why something happened – they could open a book and find out things for themselves! So what effect did all this learning and knowledge have on the world? What inventions did it lead to? And who was the greatest genius of them all?

Leonardo the genius

Leonardo was born in the town of Vinci, Italy, in 1452. He was probably the most curious man in the history of the world and the more he found out, the more he wanted to know! Unlike today, when people normally specialise in one area, Leonardo was a genius in a number of areas. He is one of the greatest ever painters, an expert scientist, a brilliant engineer, a wonderful mathematician, an excellent philosopher, a very good architect and a half-decent musician and poet! In fact, he was so good at so many different things that some people have even claimed that Leonardo was an alien from outer space! In order to stay focused, he used to write a list of things to do every day (see Source A).

SOURCE A: *This is a list copied from Leonardo's original Italian notes.*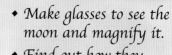

- Make glasses to see the moon and magnify it.
- Find out how they built the tower of Ferraro.
- Analyse the movement of the tongue of a woodpecker.
- Describe the jaw of a crocodile.
- Find the Frenchman who has promised to tell me the size of the sun.
- Find out how you ran on ice.

↳ SOURCE B: *This is a self-portrait of Leonardo in later life. He was a vegetarian, which was very unusual at the time, and used to buy caged birds at the market and then set them free!*

Many of his ideas concerned war and flying. He dreamed of building some of the finest weapons the world had ever seen and of designing a machine that would allow man to fly like a bird. He also designed helicopters, canals, cranes, a snorkel, a lifebelt and a submarine. He even made an alarm clock that tipped water onto a sleeping person to wake them up! Some of his sketched ideas for inventions clearly show that he thought of doing things hundreds of years before anyone else.

WISE-UP Words

Renaissance
printing press
genius

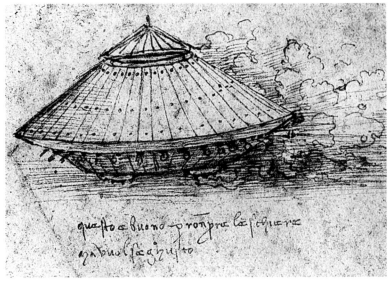

SOURCE C: *Leonardo's designs for an armoured tank and a helicopter were nearly 500 years ahead of their time!*

Work

1 Copy and complete the following sentences:

a Leonardo da Vinci was born in

_____ in 1452.

b Many people consider Leonardo to be a

_____.

c Many of his ideas are concerned with

_____ and

_____.

d Leonardo would make a _____

of new things to find out every day.

2 Why and how did the invention of the printing press lead to increased learning in Europe?

3 Look at Source A. What does this list tell you about the sort of man Leonardo was?

4 Why is this period of history often referred to as the 'Renaissance'?

5 Be like Leonardo! Design your own alarm clock that tips water on your head to wake you. Remember, no electricity!

A world reborn?

It wasn't just the ideas of Leonardo and people of the fifteenth century that were spread by the invention of the **printing press**. Old books that had been written by the Ancient Greeks and the Romans were printed and people began to rediscover knowledge that had long been lost. In the fifteenth and sixteenth centuries, these ideas were investigated and it led to fascinating discoveries in the worlds of science, medicine and engineering. This period of discovery became known as the '**Renaissance**', an Italian word meaning 'rebirth'. To many, it seemed as if their new understanding allowed them to see the world clearly for the first time. They truly felt as though they, and the rest of mankind, had been 'reborn'!

——MISSION ACCOMPLISHED?——

- Could you tell someone when Leonardo lived and three of his achievements?
- Do you know what the word 'Renaissance' means in English?
- Do you know why some people in Europe felt as though the world was being reborn?

1492 – the discovery of a New World

MISSION OBJECTIVES

- To understand how Columbus discovered a 'New World'.
- To know what new items were brought back to Europe from the New World.
- To understand how this led to the age of discovery.

Christopher Columbus had a theory. He thought that it was possible to reach China and India by sailing west, rather than having to travel east across dangerous lands. He was convinced that he could sail right around the globe and arrive in the East by sea. But although he reached land, it wasn't India. So just where had he landed? Who lived there? And what did this mean for the future of mankind?

Columbus first tried to borrow money for his journey from the kings of England, Portugal and France. They all refused. Eventually, tempted by the promise of gold and spices, Queen Isabella of Spain funded his **voyage**.

He then bought three ships, the Pinta, the Nina and the Santa Maria and hired 100 men to act as his crew. He set off on 3 August 1492.

The voyage went well for about six weeks. The crew occasionally went swimming, fished and sang together. Columbus read passages from the Bible to the men. However, by early October the crew were becoming unhappy. Water and food supplies were getting low and there was no sign of India or China. Was Columbus wrong? Perhaps the world wasn't a **sphere** after all? Were they about to fall off the edge of the world?

On 12 October, Columbus' luck changed when a lookout on the Pinta spotted land. Columbus sailed ashore and named the island San Salvador, meaning 'Holy Saviour' (it is now known as Watling Island). He spent the next few months sailing around the islands of Cuba and Haiti. He found **natives** of these islands and kidnapped six of them to take back to Queen Isabella! He also took some gold, several fish and a parrot.

Columbus returned home to a hero's welcome. He made three more trips to these new islands and also landed on the South American mainland. Until his death in 1506, Columbus still thought he'd found a new route to India or China. For many years, Native Americans were called Indians and we still call the islands he visited the 'West Indies'. Columbus had no idea that he had found a continent, America, which Europeans did not know existed. Only in later years, after explorers had found other lands, did people realise that Columbus had discovered a 'New World'.

10 October 1492

'He navigated west-south-west. They went ten miles an hour and at times twelve and sometimes seven. The men could now bear no more. They complained of the long voyage. But Admiral Columbus cheered them as best he could, holding out bright hopes of the gains they could make. He said God would keep them safe.'

↳ **SOURCE A:** *From the logbook of Columbus' ships.*

SOURCE B: *Columbus' voyage of discovery changed the history of the world.* ↱

Columbus – the first of many

Columbus' success inspired other explorers. The promise of wealth, better maps, compasses and sails meant that more people would travel the world.

- Vasco da Gama (from Portugal) – In 1498, he proved it was possible to reach India by sailing around the bottom of Africa and up the eastern coast.

- Amerigo Vespucci (from Spain) – From 1499 to 1503, he continued exploring the area where Columbus had sailed. Some people think America was named after him.

- Ferdinand Magellan (from Portugal) – On 20 September 1519, five ships and 234 men set off on a journey around the world. Magellan, the leader, died on the voyage but his crew sailed on. One ship and 18 men made it home in 1522.

- John Cabot (from England) – In 1497, he tried to reach Asia by sailing north-west. He sailed to Canada.

! FACT New goods

Explorers brought back interesting new goods from their voyages. These items had never been seen in Europe before... and were a huge success. They included tomatoes, tobacco, potatoes, turkeys and cocoa.

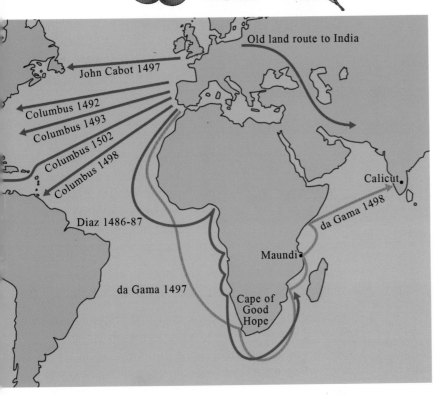

⤴ SOURCE C: *A modern map showing the routes taken by explorers, 1492–1498.*

! FACT 'I saw it first'... 'No, I saw it first'

The lookout on the Pinta, who first spotted land, was called Rodrigo. As Queen Isabella had offered a reward for the first man to sight land, Rodrigo thought he was about to receive a pension, every year for life. However, Columbus kept the money for himself... he argued that it was his voyage, so it should be his reward.

Work

1 True or false?
Write the following sentences into your books. Next to each sentence, write if it is true or false. If you believe a sentence is false, rewrite the corrected sentence underneath.
- Vasco da Gama reached India by sailing around the bottom of Italy.
- America is named after the British explorer Amerigo Vespucci.
- Ferdinand Magellan did not survive the first full journey around the world.
- John Cabot, from Scotland, discovered Australia.

2 Read Source A carefully.

a What examples can you give to show Columbus was a strong leader?

b Make up your own logbook entry for 12 October. Remember to mention Rodrigo.

3 a Where did Columbus think he had discovered in 1492?

b Was he correct?

4 Explorers were treated as heroes at this time – why do you think this was?

5 Imagine you are a ship's captain returning with 'new' goods from distant lands. Write a letter to a friend describing some of these new goods. (Good luck describing a turkey!)

___ MISSION ACCOMPLISHED? ___

- Do you know what Columbus was trying to do when he 'bumped into' the New World?
- Could you name two products that came from the New World that we now take for granted?
- Can you name an explorer other than Columbus?

Shakespeare – the most famous Englishman in history?

—————————— MISSION OBJECTIVES ——————————
- To understand how the theatre became popular in Tudor England.
- To be able to explain why William Shakespeare became the most famous Englishman in the world.

We've all heard of William Shakespeare. Most people will be able to name a few of the plays that he wrote. Many of his plays have been made into movies starring famous film stars and they are all still performed around the world today. But what has made this man so famous? Why do people still talk about him today? And why do we still study his work at school?

In medieval England, the only kind of acting that anybody saw was a mystery play. These involved local people playing out Bible stories in the streets of their town or village. This changed under the Tudors. Elizabeth thought mystery plays were a bit too Catholic. Instead, she encouraged plays that looked at things other than religion, including comedies. Actors began to tour the country performing these new plays and in London, theatres were built.

Tudor theatres

The theatres of Tudor England were very different from today's. They were circular or octagonal with two or three tiers and a stage that stuck out from one side towards the middle. The stage had a roof but no lights, so the plays had to take place in daytime. There was no scenery and the actors had no costumes, apart from hats or crowns. Spectators either stood in the **pit** – the flat ground in front of the stage – for a penny, or sat in the covered **galleries** for two pence. It wasn't just rich people who attended but people from all levels of society. They became a favourite social venue, packed with people shouting, laughing or eating.

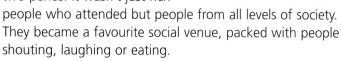
↰ SOURCE A: *The Globe Theatre.*

Superstar playwrights

The popularity of the theatre led to people earning a living by writing new plays. Many of these **playwrights** are still well known today, such as Christopher Marlowe and Ben Jonson, but by far the most famous is William Shakespeare.

Shakespeare is thought to have started writing plays in 1588. He wrote 37 in total and he appeared in some at his favourite theatre, the Globe. Like us today, the Tudor audiences probably didn't understand everything they heard on stage. There are several major reasons for this:

1 The Tudors loved to make up new words. Shakespeare himself invented about 1700 new words, such as bandit, eyeball, elbow, lonely and leapfrog. Have you ever been called a 'tower of strength' or been 'tongue tied'? Has your pencil or pen ever vanished into 'thin air'? Have you ever puzzled over something and said, 'It's all Greek to me'? Shakespeare made up all of these phrases.

2 Shakespeare wrote his plays to be acted, not just read, but he had to make sure that the audience knew exactly what was going on. This is why Shakespeare often wrote long descriptive passages to describe one scene. They tell of the time of day, the location and so on. He encouraged the audience to use their imagination.

3 English people didn't all speak the same English. Shakespeare was from Stratford-upon-Avon in the Midlands and he probably had a 'brummie' accent. In London, people spoke differently, using different words and phrases. In his plays, Shakespeare uses both kinds of English, some of which we don't use any more.

'Rich young men with nothing to do are always at the theatre. That's where they mix with the tramps, thieves and tricksters who meet there to plot their crimes. And the plays they see are full of wickedness and cheating. Those who watch are soon persuaded to copy what they see. Apprentices and servants waste their time at the theatre neglecting their work. People who should know better go there instead of to church. On top of all that, theatres can make you ill – it's easy to catch an infection in the crowd.'

↰ SOURCE B: *Letter written by the Lord Mayor of London in 1597.*

Shakespeare 'for all time'

Shakespeare's plays have been translated into every major language in the world and are constantly being performed. Why is this? It is because, although they were written over 400 years ago, they deal with human emotions, which are the same today, wherever you live in the world. In fact, Ben Jonson said that Shakespeare 'was not of an age, but for all time'.

↰ SOURCE C: *William Shakespeare.*

His play about the soldier, King Henry V, looks at courage, heroism and togetherness.

His play about Julius Caesar deals with power and betrayal.

The play Macbeth examines ambition and guilt.

His play about Romeo and Juliet is about falling in love – which has never gone out of fashion!

'Going to the theatre does young people no harm. If they don't go they might get up to worse mischief elsewhere. Most of the plays set a good example – they tell about brave actions of the men of the past. And if you do see cheats and liars on the stage, they always come to a bad end.'

SOURCE D: *Written by Thomas Nashe, a writer in 1592.*

WISE-UP Words

galleries
pit
playwright

Work

1 Why do you think fewer people visit the theatre today than in Shakespeare's time?

2 a Describe the sights, sounds and smells that a visitor to the Globe Theatre in London would have experienced in Shakespeare's time.

 b How did Tudor theatre visits compare to visiting the theatre today?

3 Design a poster advertising one of Shakespeare's plays in London in the 1560s. (Remember to include: venue, date and time of production, entry cost, name of the play and perhaps even a few lines to encourage people to attend.)

4 Write a paragraph or two explaining why Shakespeare is regarded by many as one of the world's greatest playwrights. Think about his plays, popularity, influence on the English language and talent.

MISSION ACCOMPLISHED?

• Do you know why people liked going to the theatre in Tudor times?

• Could you say why Shakespeare's plays are still so popular today?

Shakespeare or Fakespeare?

MISSION OBJECTIVES

- To understand why there is a debate over who actually wrote Shakespeare's plays and poems.
- To decide whether you are a Stratfordian or an anti-Stratfordian.

William Shakespeare is the most famous author in British history. Four hundred years after his death, millions of tourists have travelled from all over the world to visit his place of birth and his grave in Stratford-upon-Avon, England. But are they all visiting the wrong place? Ever since Shakespeare's death, people have repeatedly questioned whether the Stratford man was really responsible for the works of Shakespeare. But why is this? Who do they think wrote them instead? And has the whole world been fooled by the most amazing hoax in history?

Nobody denies that there was a man called William Shakespeare who was born in Stratford-upon-Avon in 1564. There is no argument that he got married aged 18, had three children and moved to London to become an actor. He is listed among actors who performed twice for Queen Elizabeth and his name appears as a shareholder of the Globe Theatre. But what people argue about is whether this man was responsible for writing plays such as *Romeo and Juliet* and *Macbeth*. Those who believe he wrote the plays are known as **Stratfordians**, and those who doubt that he did are called **anti-Stratfordians**. Look at the following sources and decide which side you're on!

'Unlike other writers of the period, not a single manuscript (original copy of a play) or letter exists in Shakespeare's own handwriting. Nothing survives of a literary nature that connects William of Stratford, the man, with any of the 'Shakespeare' works.'

↳ SOURCE A: *Matthew Cossolotto, President of the Shakespeare Oxford Society.*

'Shakespeare's name appeared on the very first printed editions of the works and other writers in his lifetime credit Shakespeare with being the author. Nobody ever claimed the plays were written by someone else during Shakespeare's lifetime.'

↳ SOURCE C: *David Kathman, an American scholar who edits a website about Shakespeare.*

'There are no official records that state Shakespeare was a writer, but there are about 70 documents that state he was an actor or a money-lender. There are only six examples of his signature – and they all spell his name differently.'

↳ SOURCE B: *William Leahy, Head of Shakespeare Authorship Studies, Brunel University.*

'Shakespeare's background needs clearing up – the idea that he was a poor man and a commoner is wrong. His father was the mayor of Stratford, which was a thriving market town. He came from a decent background and his education at Stratford Grammar School rivalled any education today.'

↳ SOURCE D: *Stuart Hampton-Reeves, of the British Shakespeare Society.*

'Shakespeare could have gone to Stratford Grammar School but no records exist to prove that and, even if he did, it would have been only for six years.'

↳ SOURCE E: *William Leahy, Head of Shakespeare Authorship Studies, Brunel University.*

'It is a bit strange that nothing is mentioned about his hometown yet 13 of his plays are set in Italy.'

↳ SOURCE F: *William Leahy, Head of Shakespeare Authorship Studies, Brunel University.*

'Italian culture and literature were widespread in all of Elizabethan literature and drama – not just Shakespeare. There were many sources for any intelligent Elizabethan to use to find out about Italy.'

↳ SOURCE G: *David Kathman, an American scholar who edits a website about Shakespeare.*

SOURCE H: *David Kathman.*

'William Shakespeare of Stratford-upon-Avon was an actor in the company that performed the plays of William Shakespeare, and was also a sharer in the theatre in which the plays were presented. To anyone with a logical mind, it follows that this William Shakespeare of Stratford-upon-Avon was also the writer of the plays and poems that bear his name. He is the man with the right name, at the right time and at the right place.'

SOURCE I: *Matthew Cossolotto, President of the Shakespeare Oxford Society.*

'Shakespeare returned to Stratford in his 40s, bought a big house, traded in grain and property and died in 1616. There was no large funeral, no commemoration in London and no poems written in honour. He didn't leave a single book in his will and his daughters lived and died illiterate (unable to read or write).'

WISE-UP Words

anti-Stratfordians
Stratfordians

Work

1 Write a brief description of each source in the correct column.

Stratfordian	Anti-Stratfordian

2 Are you a Stratfordian or an anti-Stratfordian? Write a paragraph explaining your decision.

3 Do you think it matters if Shakespeare of Stratford was the true author of the works of Shakespeare? Give reasons for your answer.

Who was it then?

Over the years, people have claimed that a number of different people were the real genius behind Shakespeare. Today, most anti-Stratfordians believe that the works were written by Edward de Vere, who lived from 1550–1604. He was a nobleman who had two university degrees by the time he was 17, travelled widely and was famed for his poems even though none were published in his name. According to anti-Stratfordians, he was unable to publish plays in his own name as many of the characters were based on real people in Elizabeth's court, including the Queen herself! If the plays were published under a false name, like William Shakespeare, no one could put the blame on de Vere!

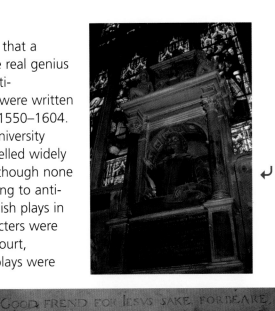

SOURCE J: *This bust of Shakespeare was placed in Holy Trinity Church six years after Shakespeare's death. Anti-Stratfordians have claimed that it was only after his death that Shakespeare was thought of as a playwright.*

SOURCE K: *The final two lines on Shakespeare's grave say 'Blest the man who spares these stones, and curst be he that moves my bones.' Some people have questioned whether this was meant to stop people investigating further.*

SOURCE L: *Matthew Cossolotto, President of the Shakespeare Oxford Society.*

'Many of the plays contain characters' and details that relate directly to De Vere's life. They show an intimate knowledge of a wide range of subjects, including the law, Italy, foreign languages, heraldry, music, navigation, court manners and gossip, and warfare. De Vere's known educational background, foreign travels and life experiences match the knowledge base shown in Shakespeare's plays and poems.'

SOURCE M: *Sigmund Freud, the world-famous psychologist.*

'I am almost convinced that the assumed name (William Shakespeare) conceals the personality of Edward de Vere, Earl of Oxford. The man of Stratford seems to have nothing at all to justify his claim, whereas Oxford has almost everything.'

SOURCE N: *Stuart Hampton-Reeves of the British Shakespeare Society.*

'Where's the document that links De Vere or anyone else to the plays? It's non-existent.'

MISSION ACCOMPLISHED?

- Could you explain why some people doubt whether Shakespeare of Stratford wrote the works of Shakespeare?
- Have you decided if you are a Stratfordian or an anti-Stratfordian?

TASK 1 Mapping the world

Sources A and B show two maps. Source A was drawn in 1489 and shows what Europeans thought about the size of the world at that time. Source B is a modern world map. Study the maps carefully and answer the questions that follow.

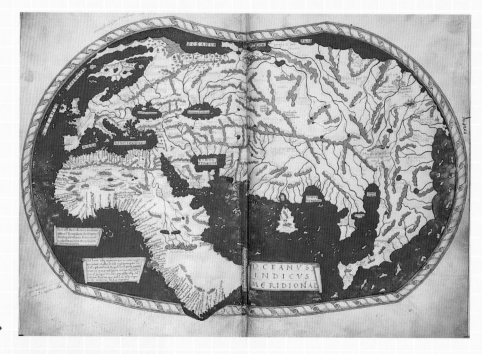

SOURCE A:
Map of the world drawn by Henricus Martellus in 1489. ↱

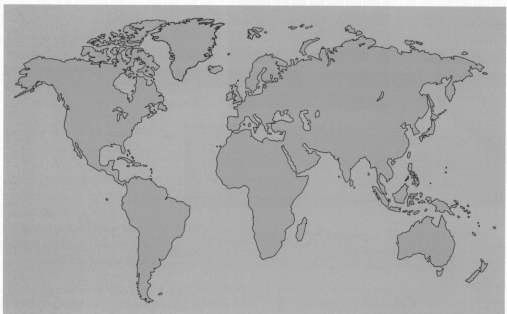

↰ SOURCE B: *A modern world map.*

a What major continents and oceans featured on the modern world map are not found on the Martellus map of 1489?

b Why do you think the major continents and oceans aren't found on the older map?

c Make a list of reasons why we know so much more about the world than the Tudors did.

TASK 2 Punctuation practice

The passage below doesn't make sense. It needs capital letters, commas and full stops. Some words are spelled incorrectly. (In total, five words are spelt incorrectly.)

Copy the passage, making corrections as you write.

leonardo da vinci was a genious he tried hard to be the best at everything he did he filled his days with things to do such as studying fossels oil painting glass making and wepon building leonardo was especially concerned with a dream of flying and dreamed of designing a machine that wood allow a man to fly like a bird the period in which leonardo lived was known as the rennasance.

Painting of Henry VIII, his three children and Jane Seymour.

TASK 3 Who's who?

a Can you work out who is in the picture above?

b Write a sentence or two about each of the people pictured with Henry VIII.

c Could all five people have stood together to have this picture painted? Think carefully about your answer.

TASK 4 Making notes

Note making is an important skill. To do it successfully you must pick out any key words in each of the sentences. In other words, without these key words the sentence would make no sense. The first one has been done for you.

a In 1485, Henry VII was crowned the King of England. The key words are 1485, Henry VII, crowned and King of England.

b At this time most people thought that the world was flat.

c The only areas that were really known about were Europe, the Holy Land, northern Africa and the Eastern lands, such as China and India.

d By 1500, many explorers had read the stories of the famous adventurer Marco Polo.

e Ptolemy, a Greek writer, wrote a book entitled 'Geography' in which he talked of the theory that the world was not flat but shaped like a ball.

f Several brave explorers, including Christopher Columbus, became excited by the stories of adventure and decided to sail further than they had sailed before.

g They were helped by accurate compasses, top quality sails and good rudders.

TOP TIP: Note making is an important skill to use during revision time. Can you make notes on any other paragraphs in your books?

TASK 5 King Henry the Great

Henry VIII didn't ever really expect to be king. In fact, his dad, Henry VII, thought his youngest son would end up with a career in the Church. However, when Henry's older brother, Arthur died suddenly in 1502, young Prince Henry was next in line for the throne. So was he fit to be king?

Look through all the comments below about the young Prince Henry. You will notice that the comments vary: some praise him, others criticise him. Your task is to write a balanced account of Henry, making sure you answer the question: 'Was Henry fit to be king?'

- He is tall and handsome.
- He is a talented musician.
- He is a super sportsman. He is very good at archery, tennis, wrestling and jousting.
- He enjoys spending money, whereas his father is very careful with it.
- He wasn't brought up to be king.
- He speaks many foreign languages including French, Latin and Greek.
- He is desperate to fight in wars and would love to win important battles. He calls war 'the sport of kings'.
- He is very stubborn, just wanting to do whatever he wants all the time.
- He loves playing jokes on people.
- He has lots of energy; when hunting, he can wear out up to five horses a day.
- He enjoys dancing and having thought-provoking conversations.

TOP TIP: Your aim is to provide a balanced answer, so you will need to use connectives such as, 'however', 'on the other hand' and 'in contrast'.

A portrait of Henry VIII showing him in his late twenties.

COULD YOU GET JUSTICE IN TUDOR ENGLAND?

The topic of crime and punishment is big news. The latest crime figures, the nastiest murder trials and the state of our prisons are issues that are always on our TV screens, on the radio and in newspapers and magazines. As a result, we know quite a lot about law and order in today's society. But what was the state of law and order in Tudor times? What types of criminals roamed around the country? How were these criminals caught and punished? Indeed, how could you get justice in Tudor England?

1: 'In terror of the tramp'

MISSION OBJECTIVES
- To understand how some of the poorer people in Tudor England tried to make money.
- To understand why these so-called 'sturdy beggars' were treated so brutally.

The origin of the sturdy beggar

The number of poor people increased in Tudor England. The first Tudor King, Henry VII, banned his rich barons from keeping private armies, so lots of men lost their jobs as soldiers. To make matters worse, many large landowners started to keep sheep on their land rather than allow tenants to hire it and grow crops. This meant fewer jobs, as tenant farmers and their workers and families had to leave their manors to fend for themselves. Later, when Henry VIII closed all the monasteries, the increasing number of poor people couldn't even go to the local monks for their handouts.

All this led to an increase in the number of poor people wandering the streets looking for food and shelter. These **vagabonds**, as the Tudors called them, were a mixture of unemployed soldiers and farmers, women and children, the old and sick. A small minority, who were fit enough to look for work, found that crime was an easier way for them to make a living. In Tudor England, this rough, tough, devious bunch of vagabond con men were also known as '**sturdy beggars**'.

Types of sturdy beggar

In 1567, a man named Thomas Harman wrote a best-selling book warning against the dangers of sturdy beggars. He described 23 different types of these tricksters, some of whom are detailed here.

The Bristler
The Bristler would use specially weighted dice ('bristles' were loaded or crooked dice), which would land on whichever number the Bristler chose.

The Counterfeit Crank
Dressed in old, grubby clothes, he would pretend to have violent fits. He would often suck soap so that he frothed at the mouth! The worse he shook, the more money he hoped to attract because people would feel sorry for him.

The Clapper Dudgeon

He would cut his skin to make it bleed and tie dirty rags over the wounds to make it look even worse. He hoped people would feel sorry for him and give him money so he could get medical attention.

Tom O'Bedlam

He would pretend to be mad and follow people around. Often he would carry a stick with a piece of meat attached to the end or spend hours barking like a dog or stuffing chicken heads into his ears. Why do you think people gave him money?

The Baretop Trickster

She would flash at a man in the street and ask him to buy her a meal. The man, thinking he might get to have sex with the woman, would accompany her to a nearby house… where a vicious gang would be waiting to rob him!

↵ **SOURCE A:** *A picture of Baretop Tricksters that appeared in a warning leaflet in the 1500s.*

! FACT **Nice job!** In 1566, London beggar Nicholas Jennings is caught with a bag of blood that he uses to paint fake injuries on his head. In a day he made the equivalent of two weeks' wages for an ordinary worker.

The Cutpurse – a pickpocket who would secretly creep up behind you, cut a hole in your pocket or bag and steal the contents.

The Angler – fixed a hook to a long stick and stole clothes from washing lines.

The Dummerer – pretended to be deaf and dumb, hoping people would feel sorry for him.

Priggers of Prancers – horse thieves.

Rufflers – ex-soldiers who beat people up to get their purses.

↳ SOURCE B: *Some other sturdy beggars, as featured in Harman's 1567 book about them.*

! FACT What are you on about?

Sturdy beggars developed their own language, a kind of slang known as canting. They used it to speak secretly to other thieves on busy streets. Amazingly, some 'canting' words managed to work their way into everyday use. For example, booze (meaning 'alcohol'), peck (meaning 'food' – ever said you were 'peckish'?), duds (meaning 'clothes'), lift (meaning 'steal') and beak (meaning 'police' or the 'law') will still be recognisable to some of you today!

SOURCE C: *From William Harrison's Description of England, published in 1577.*

'The vagabond abide nowhere but runneth up and down from place to place. Idle beggars make corrosives and apply them to the fleshy parts of their bodies ... to raise pitiful sores and move the hearts of passers-by so they will bestow large gifts upon them. How liberally they beg, what forcible speech that makes me think that punishment is more suitable for them than generosity or gifts.

They are all thieves and extortionists. They lick the sweat from the true labourers' brows and take from the godly poor what is due to them. It is not yet 60 years since this trade began but how it has prospered since that time is easy to judge for they are now supposed to amount to 10 000... Moreover, they have devised a language among themselves which they name canting such as none but themselves are able to understand.'

As the number of sturdy beggars increased, they became one of the ruling classes' biggest headaches. They were thought to be behind all sorts of crime and, in 1531, the government took firm action.

Whilst some old and sick people were given a special licence to beg, those who weren't given one would be whipped until their 'bodies be bloody' if they were caught out on the streets. If they were caught again, they had a 2.5cm hole bored through the ear, whilst a third conviction meant death by hanging! At one point, during Edward VI's reign, any person found begging even ONCE would be made a slave for two years and branded on the forehead with the letter V (for vagabond)!

Gradually, it became clear that most vagabonds were not a threat to law and order at all. Instead, they were just genuinely poor and unemployed people who were looking for work. In the late 1500s, various laws were passed that ordered each district or parish to provide money for the poor. Queen Elizabeth I went one step further in 1601 when she backed the first official Poor Law. This said that each area should tax wealthy local people and use the money to provide work and support for the old and sick. The law still maintained that anyone who refused to work should be whipped and then put in a **House of Correction**. There, they had to make things that were later sold. Even their children were taken from them and given jobs. Not surprisingly, some beggars were so afraid of the House of Correction that some cities reported a drop of 90% in the number of people wandering the streets!

'29 March 1573. At Harrow on the Hill in Middlesex, on the said day, John Allan, Elizabeth Turner, Humphrey Foxe, Henry Bower and Agnes Fort, being over 14 years and having no lawful means of livelihood, were declared vagabonds. Sentenced to be flogged and burned through the right ear.'

↳ SOURCE D: *From Middlesex County Records, 1573.*

! FACT What about prisons?

There were prisons in Tudor and Stuart times but they tended to be a place where people were held before their trial or while awaiting punishment. Unlike today, it was very rarely used as a punishment in its own right!

SOURCE E: *How the Tudors treated sturdy beggars.*

Date of law	King or Queen	Action
1495	Henry VII	Beggars to go in stocks for three days, then sent back to their birth-place or previous residence.
1531	Henry VIII	Some 'worthy' poor, old and sick given licence to beg. Others should be whipped and sent back to where they came from. Harsher punishments for repeat offenders.
1547	Edward VI	Beggars whipped and branded with a V on forehead (for vagabond). Also to be made a slave for two years. If they offend again or try to escape, they will be executed (this law remained in force for three years before it was changed back to the 1531 law because it was viewed as too severe).
1601	Elizabeth I	Local taxes should help the poor. Poor people who refuse to work should be imprisoned. Beggars will still be whipped until they bleed and sent back to where they came from.

WISE-UP Words

canting
House of Correction
sturdy beggar   vagabond

! FACT Trial and retribution

Some offences were dealt with by a local magistrate (trial for less serious crimes are still held in magistrates' courts today). Most guilty people were either fined or faced some sort of public humiliation, such as the stocks, pillory or ducking stool. Criminals accused of more serious crimes were often sent to a local jail until one of the king (or queen's) judges visited a local large town and the trial could go ahead. At trial, the prisoner had to conduct their own defence in front of the judge and jury.

Work

1 a Why did the number of poor people increase in Tudor England?

b What was a 'sturdy beggar'?

2 a Write down three examples of how sturdy beggars were punished if caught.

b Why do you think Tudor kings and queens treated sturdy beggars so brutally?

3 Look at Source E. In what ways did the Poor Law of 1601 differ from earlier laws that dealt with poorer people?

4 a Here are five ways that sturdy beggars were punished: whipped, branded, hanged, put in a House of Correction, made into a slave. Write down the one you think was the most suitable punishment and explain why you chose it.

b Why don't you think we punish poor people and beggars today?

5 The year is 1543 and you work as a printer in a large town. The Mayor has asked you to design a leaflet warning visitors about the dangers of sturdy beggars. Your warning leaflet should include details about some (or all) of the sturdy beggars mentioned on these pages and about how they might try to trick someone.

↵ SOURCE F: *A beggar being whipped through the streets in 1577.*

MISSION ACCOMPLISHED?

• Do you know the difference between a counterfeit crank and a clapper dudgeon?

• Could you give three examples of how Tudor kings and queens tried to deal with sturdy beggars?

In Tudor and Stuart England, crimes were punished in much the same way as they had been in the Middle Ages. The stocks and pillory were still used regularly but fining a criminal was still the most common way of punishing minor crimes. For serious offences, there were still very harsh punishments. In 1533, a cook was boiled to death in a cauldron for trying to poison the Bishop of Rochester (judges were perhaps trying to make the punishment fit the crime!).

2: What did the Scottish Boot, the Juda Cradle and the Spanish Donkey have in common?

_____ MISSION OBJECTIVES _____

• To understand why and how torture was used in England during this time.

Some towns still had watchmen and constables to look out for crooks, and Justices of the Peace tried to investigate crimes, gather information and hold trials. However, these government-appointed men were also busy with other duties, such as looking after roads and bridges, checking alehouses and reporting people who continually failed to attend church! As a result, the government sometimes used other ways of getting information, catching criminals and foiling plots. One way was to employ spies but this was time-consuming and costly (you had to pay the spy of course). A much more brutal solution was to use torture! So what were some of Tudor England's more brutal torture techniques?

The Rack

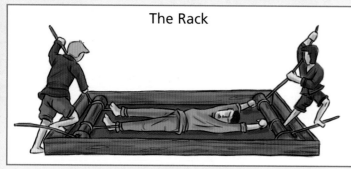

How did it work?
A prisoner was stretched for hours on end. Often, their tendons and ligaments would tear and their shoulders would become dislocated.
Fact: There was only one rack in the whole of England, which was kept in the Tower of London. One famous Tudor rack torturer boasted that most of his victims were a foot longer by the time he had finished with them.

The Press

How did it work?
A prisoner would lay under strong wooden or metal boards whilst heavy stones were placed upon them. If a prisoner failed to own up to their crimes, another heavy rock could be placed on them.
Fact: One press operator once boasted that he knew his victim would not be able to hold out much longer 'as soon as I heard his chest crack'.

The Spanish Donkey

How did it work?
Weights were attached to a prisoner's legs whilst they sat astride the wooden 'donkey'. More weights were applied until the prisoner confessed.
Fact: A torture first used in Spain, the idea was to destroy a victim's genitals!

The Juda Cradle

How did it work?
A victim was hung above a cone pyramid and then lowered onto it. The sharp tip of the cone was forced up into the area between the prisoner's legs.
Fact: Visitors are told about this torture on a tour of the Tower of London; it usually gets the biggest gasps!

The Scottish Boot

How did it work?
A prisoner's foot was placed in a heavy metal boot and wooden wedges would be hammered down the sides. Gradually, the leg and anklebones would be crushed and splintered into pieces.
Fact: A similar contraption called the Copper Boot was sometimes used. For this torture, molten red-hot lead was poured into a boot, giving the victim terrible burns.

Skeffington's Irons

How did it work?
Specially designed to keep the prisoner in a very uncomfortable position. Either they owned up to the crime… or their back was broken.
Fact: This torture was named after its inventor, Leonard Skeffington, who was once head torturer for Henry VIII.

'... Then they took me to a big upright pillar. Driven into the top of it were iron staples for supporting heavy weights. They then put my wrists in iron gauntlets [gloves] and ordered me to climb some wooden steps.

My arms were lifted up and an iron bar was passed through the rings of one gauntlet, then through the staple and the rings of the second gauntlet. They fastened the bar with a pin. Removing the steps, they left me hanging with my hands and arms fastened above my head. The tips of my toes, however, still touched the ground and they had to dig away at the earth from under them.

I began to pray. The gentlemen asked me whether I was willing to confess now.'

↳ **SOURCE A:** *Father Gerard, a Catholic priest, was tortured in the Tower of London in 1597.*

Work

1 a What were the two main methods used to get information in Tudor England?

b Why did the Tudors favour torture over the use of spies?

c List as many reasons as you can to explain why we don't torture suspected criminals today.

2 Look at Source A.

a In your own words, describe how Father Gerard is being tortured.

b Why did earth have to be dug away from under the prisoner's feet?

3 Most of this torture equipment still survives today, kept on display in the Tower of London. Design an information leaflet for a young schoolchild to use as a guide on a torture chamber tour. Include:

- colourful pictures of the torture instruments;
- facts about how they worked;
- a background to torture;
- an imaginative title, for example, 'The Tower's Terrible Torture Guide'.

___ MISSION ACCOMPLISHED? ___

- Can you explain why torture was used in Tudor England?
- Do you know the difference between the rack and the press?

Who's who?

_____ MISSION OBJECTIVES _____

• To identify the four main groups who made up Tudor society.

We are all different. We all look, dress and behave differently. We don't all have the same amount of money either. It was just the same in Tudor England. You could place people into groups. Historians often use the word class instead of group. In 1586, a man called William Harrison wrote a book called 'Description of England'. In it, he divided people into four classes. He wrote, 'We in England divide our people into four groups: gentlemen, citizens, yeomen and labourers.' So what did he mean?

Read about the four groups mentioned in Harrison's book. Later on you will be asked to match each group to a house, a description of their life and a picture.

Now study the following photographs, descriptions and portraits. Soon you will have to match a home, a description and a picture to each of the groups of people (gentlemen, citizens, yeomen and labourers).

Who were the **gentlemen**?

These guys were rich. Some were very, very rich like the dukes and earls. They lived in huge country houses with lots of rooms in which to hold dinner parties, dances, plays and music concerts. They employed servants to look after them. Other gentlemen were not quite so rich but still lived in large houses with plenty of land. Gentlemen (and their wives and families) made up about 5% of the population.

Who were the **citizens**?

These people lived in towns and were still rich. Some made money from buying and selling goods, such as wool, jewellery, food, wine or cloth. These men were sometimes called **merchants**. They lived in fine town houses and had servants. They made up about 5% of the population.

Who were the **yeomen**?

They were farmers. They either owned their own land or rented land from a gentleman. They often lived in a medium-sized farmhouse and made quite a good living from farming crops (wheat or barley, for example) or cattle, pigs, or sheep. They employed people to work on their farms and some yeomen even had servants. Yeomen and their families made up about 30% of the population.

Who were the **labourers**?

These people were similar in status to the peasants of the Middle Ages. If they lived in the country – and most did – they would work on a farm. Some had their own small piece of land to grow their own vegetables and keep a few chickens. Some labourers lived in towns and might have worked as carpenters, tailors, shoemakers or bricklayers. Labourers made up about 60% of the population.

↖ SOURCE A: *Home A.*

↳ SOURCE B: *Home B.*

SOURCE C: *Home C.* ↳

↑ SOURCE D: *Home D.*

DESCRIPTION 1

'He eats well: bread, beer and beef, good food... full bellyfuls. He works hard: making hay, shearing corn, his workers are happy to farm for him.'

DESCRIPTION 2

'His house has walls of earth, a low thatched roof, few rooms... a hole in the wall to let out smoke... he is very poor and has to labour hard for his living.'

Picture 1

Picture 3

Picture 2

DESCRIPTION 3

'Every day he wears silks, velvets, satins and such like. He once gave away a pair of perfumed gloves with 24 small gold buttons, in each button a small diamond.'

DESCRIPTION 4

'He brought back with him wine, olive oil, currants, silk, clothes and dates. He sold them to a man who then sold them in London.'

Picture 4

FACT The poorest of the poor

Even lower than the poorest labourers were the **paupers** – people who had no jobs and relied on charity. Some paupers were given permission to beg and wore special badges to show this. Others went to their local church to collect 'relief' – a few pennies to buy clothes or bread. Local people were taxed to pay for this.

In 1601, a **Poor Law** put the paupers into four categories. Each group was treated differently:

1 Pauper children – given work.

2 Sick paupers – looked after in special homes.

3 Fit paupers – given work (they received food and drink as payment).

4 Lazy, idle paupers – whipped, then sent to a House of Correction (a place where they were forced to work, then their products werea sold).

Again, people were taxed to pay for the relief provided through the Poor Law.

WISE-UP Words

class
citizen
gentleman
labourer
merchant
pauper
Poor Law
yeoman

__MISSION ACCOMPLISHED?__

• Can you explain the main differences between rich and poor Tudors?

Work

1 a In your own words, explain the meaning of the following:

gentleman • citizen • yeoman • labourer

• pauper

2 a Copy this chart carefully.

b Complete the chart by looking closely at the information on these pages. Match the descriptions and pictures to the correct group or 'class' of people.

c Now choose one of the sets of sources you have matched together and explain how you made your decision, for example:

• I think picture _____ shows a gentleman because…

• Home _____ would belong to a gentleman because…

• Description _____ is that of a gentleman because…

Class	Which **home** do you think he lived in? (A–D)	Which **description** matches him?	What does he look like? Choose from pictures 1–4.
Gentlemen Citizens Yeomen Labourers			

What were Tudor schools like?

MISSION OBJECTIVES

- To remember at least five facts about education in Tudor England.
- To understand how today's classrooms are different from those long ago.

Have you ever had an adult tell you how tough school was in 'their day'? Bet you have! They would have probably told you about the scary teachers, how long detentions were and the horrible food. In fact, some of you sitting in a classroom today probably think your school life is really tough – so it's a good job you didn't go to school in Tudor times.

A Tudor child's education often depended on how wealthy their father was. It wasn't free to attend school, so poor families couldn't afford the school fees. As a result, poor children would probably start work when they were five or six years old.

Richer families might send her children to a **grammar school**, so called because they taught mainly Latin and Greek grammar. Latin was the language used by businessmen and merchants throughout Europe – so any ambitious father would make sure their child was taught at one of Britain's best grammar schools, like Rugby or Harrow.

The following scene is based on a classroom at a school near Chester called Banbury Grammar School, which opened in 1594. Nearly every large town had a grammar school in Queen Elizabeth's reign.

! FACT You've never had it so good!
Schools closed for two weeks at Christmas and two weeks at Easter. A school week was often Monday to Saturday too – and there were no summer holidays.

+ Hungry for MORE
Using your local library, find out details of the oldest school in your area.
- How old is it?
- How has the school changed over the years?
- Are there any things that have stayed the same and provide us with evidence of the past?
- Are there any famous ex-students?

WISE-UP Words

birch   hornbook
grammar school
quill pen

SOURCE A: *A typical school timetable for a day. Lessons must have been dull – no computers, televisions, Internet or interactive whiteboards. And a lot of the lessons had to be learned off by heart.* ↱

6:00am – Day starts – Registration
6:15am – Prayers
7:00am – Latin Grammar
9:00am – Maths
11:00am – Lunch (bread, beef, dried fruit, ale)
12:00pm – Greek Grammar
2:00pm – Essays
3:00pm – Divinity (Religious Studies)
4:00pm – Homework given out
4:45pm – Prayers/Bible reading
5:00pm – Hometime

KEY

1 SCHOOL RULES: Tudor schools were very strict. You could be beaten for being late, not learning to spell properly, swearing, making fun of another student, forgetting books or gambling. Are some of your school rules similar to the ones Tudor children had to follow?

2 THE BIRCH: A bundle of **birch** twigs or even a whip were used to hit children. A punishment session would be held once a week! Some school badges actually showed boys being caned. Why do you think that this type of punishment has stopped in the last 50 years?

3 A PORTRAIT: A painting of the King, Queen or the man who founded the school would often be displayed in the classroom. Does your school display any portraits or photographs of any important people?

4 PRINTED BOOKS: Each student was expected to bring their own Bible at Banbury Grammar School. Why do you think that many of the other books were kept behind the teacher?

5 GIRLS IN SCHOOL: Girls were allowed to study at Banbury until they were nine or they had learned to read. It wasn't common to see girls in a classroom and many were educated at home. Some free places were also allocated to boys who were poor but clever.

6 LESSON TIME: What lesson do you think is taking place here? What makes you think this? Children wrote with a **quill pen**, made from a feather, and often read out loud from a **hornbook** (it looked like a wooden bat). What else do you think it could be used for? One side would have the alphabet and the Lord's Prayer on it. The other side was left blank and was used to practise writing or maths on.

7 TEACHER: Sometimes called a schoolmaster. Teachers were always men and could be very strict. In one school, a particularly strict teacher used to whip students every morning in winter… just to warm himself up!

8 TOYS: Balls, spinning tops and hoops were used at break times. The students would usually have two or three breaks each day, bringing bread, beef and beer with them from home. The day would begin at 6:00am and home time could be 12 hours later. Parents had to buy candles in the winter so their children could read – and they had to buy any additional books they might need too! In fact, a year's books might cost over £10, which was about as much as the teacher earned each year!

School rules

You will be beaten for
· Arriving late.
· Not learning a passage from the Bible off by heart.
· Forgetting your books.
· Hitting another pupil.
· Playing with dice or cards.
· Going to an alehouse at dinnertime.
· Hitting another pupil.
· Losing your school cap.
· Making fun or another pupil.
· Stealing, swearing or lying.
· Wearing a dagger or bringing a stick or a bat to school – only meat knifes allowed.

↰ **SOURCE B:** *Genuine school rules from England, including Manchester Grammar school and Oundle school.*

Work

1 Write two sentences to describe each of the following:
   birch • quill pen • hornbook

2 Why did so few poor children go to school in Tudor times?

3 Make a list of five similarities and five differences between your school and a school in Tudor times.

4 'A day in the life of (insert name) at (insert name) Grammar School.'

   Imagine you are a student at the Tudor version of your school. Using the information provided on these pages, write a diary entry describing a typical day at your school. Use Source A to help you.

5 Look at Source B.

   a Which of the 'offences' on the list would you not be punished for in your school?

   b Explain why you wouldn't be punished?

MISSION ACCOMPLISHED?

• Can you explain how Tudor schools differ from the schools we go to today?

How did people have fun in Tudor England?

―――――――――――― MISSION OBJECTIVES ――――――――――――
• To understand how and why Tudor entertainment differs from the types of entertainment we enjoy today.

There was no television or radio in Tudor times. People couldn't go to the cinema, play on a computer game or listen to CDs. Instead, they had to make their own entertainment. You will easily recognise some of the games and sports… others might leave you reaching for the sick bucket!

Go to public executions: Tudor people loved to see criminals being killed. Poorer criminals were hanged; richer ones were beheaded with a sword. In London, spectators complained when one hangman executed 20 people at once – they were not happy because they wanted the criminals to be killed one at a time so they could see the expression on each prisoner's face!

Join in with the football match: One village or town would take on another. The ball (a pig's bladder full of sawdust and peas) would be carried, kicked and thrown across the land between the two villages. The winning 'team' was the one that got the ball into the centre of the other village. In 1602, a spectator wrote, 'The players go home as if they have been at war – bleeding heads, bones broken and out of joint, and such bruises as serve to shorten their days.'

Play Cudgels or Shin-hacks: Two simple games for two players.

To play **Cudgels** – two people stand opposite each other, each holding a heavy stick. They then take it in turns to hit each other. The person left standing wins.

To play **Shin-hacks** – two people stand opposite each other in their biggest, heaviest boots. They take it in turns to kick each other as hard as they can. The person left standing wins.

'A large bear on a long rope was tied to a stake. The many great English bulldogs were brought in and first shown to the bear, which afterwards they baited one after another. The excellence and guts of such bulldogs were shown, for although they were much struck and mauled by the bear, they did not give in, but had to be pulled off by sheer force and their mouths kept open with long sticks with a broad iron –piece fixed to the top.'

↳ **SOURCE A:** *A 1599 report describes bear baiting.*

WISE-UP Words

strolling players
blood sports
Cudgels
Shin-hacks

Watch the strolling players: Groups of actors travelled from village to village and acted out well-known stories or plays. They also carried news and gossip. Often, they were joined by acrobats, jugglers, musicians and puppeteers. Plays soon became so popular that special theatres were built. William Shakespeare wrote plays that were performed in the Globe Theatre in London.

Bet on blood sports: A bear or a bull would be tied to a post and attacked by a pack of wild dogs. Sometimes two cocks or chickens would be forced to attack each other after having their beaks sharpened and metal blades attached to their legs. People would bet on the results. Some successful bears, such as Harry Hunks, Tom Lincoln and Blind Robin, became as famous as some footballers and pop stars are today.

All the fun of the fair: There were no roller coaster rides or arcade games. Instead, a fair was a large noisy market full of goods to buy, food to eat and entertainment to watch (or join in with). Fire-eaters, tightrope walkers, sword fighting and dog racing were all popular, as were most of the other sports and entertainment on this page.

↳ **SOURCE B:** *The 'Cotswold Olympick Games' started in 1604 and were held every year during Whitsun.*

Ordinary people had tough lives and worked long hours in Tudor England. So, when they had any spare time, they would set out in search of serious fun! Drinking, singing, playing games and dancing were as popular back then as they are now… and even lead one foreign visitor in the 1600s to write that 'no nation beats the English in their variety of sports and entertainment'.

! FACT Famous fairs
• London – Cloth Fair
• Nottingham – Goose Fair
• Birmingham – Gingerbread Fair
• Gloucester – 'Cotswold Olimpicks', a week of noise, food, fun and fighting.
Why not try to find out about one of the above? The Goose Fair is still going strong today.

'It does seem strange that the Tudor people who so much admired beauty in music, poetry, drama and architecture should have taken such delight in cruel, blood thirsty 'sports' which involved the torture of animals.'

↵ SOURCE C: *A modern historian writing about the Tudor people's love of such 'spirits' as bear-baiting and cockfighting.*

'There were a great many inns, taverns and beer gardens scattered about the city, where much amusement may be had in eating, drinking, fiddling and the rest.'

↵ SOURCE D: *A German tourist describing Tudor London. Having a beer at a local 'pub' was just as popular in Tudor England as it is with some people today.*

↳ SOURCE E: *People enjoying themselves in 1485.*

!FACT Royal sports stars

Kings and queens enjoyed sport too. Henry VIII enjoyed tennis, archery, skittles and wrestling. In 1520, he challenged King Francis of France to a wrestling match. The two men actually wrestled each other but Henry fell over and lost after a few minutes. He was so humiliated that he claimed he had been tripped up!

Mary Queen of Scots had her own billiards table and also enjoyed the odd game of golf – so did Charles I, who played in a field near Newcastle a few months before he had his head chopped off.

SOURCE F: *In Tudor times, drinking, singing and dancing were always popular. Dice, cards, draughts, chess and dominoes were popular too – so was a basic board game called 'Merelles' or 'Five Men's Morris'.* ↱

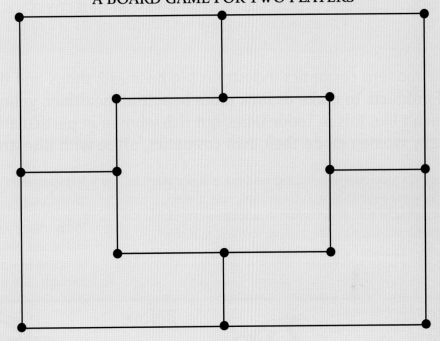

FIVE MEN'S MORRIS
A BOARD GAME FOR TWO PLAYERS

Rules:
1 Draw the board pictured above on a large piece of card.
2 Both players have five counters or coins.
3 Each player takes it in turn to place a counter on a dot.
4 The aim is to get three counters in row or sequence.
5 Each player tries to block the other from making a run of three.
6 If, when all the 10 counters are on the board, neither player has won, the counters can be slid, one step at a time. A player can only slide to an open dot, one move at a time.
7 The first to get three in a row is the winner.

Work

1 a Which forms of Tudor entertainment seem unpleasant or cruel to us, or have been made illegal today?

 b Why do you think some of the sports and entertainments have been banned?

2 a Where does the word 'holiday' come from?

 b Why would a band of strolling players coming to town be such a big event in Tudor times?

 c In what ways is the modern game of football different from that played in Tudor times?

3 Design a poster advertising a local fair in Tudor times. Remember to include the day of the fair (it must be on the day of a religious festival) and details of the entertainment taking place.

4 Look at Source E. People would have enjoyed themselves like this in 1485. With a partner, list as many of the games and activities that you can see. You should be able to spot at least eight, including the boy tied up in a knot!

!FACT Time for fun

Most games, sports and festivals would take place on holy days such as Christmas, May Day and Midsummer Eve. People would attend church services in the morning and have fun later on in the day. The word 'holiday' comes from the words 'holy day'.

— MISSION ACCOMPLISHED? —

• Can you accurately describe three types of Tudor entertainment not enjoyed today and explain why they have been banned or are not practiced anymore?

Fashion victims

_____ MISSION OBJECTIVES _____

• To understand what some rich Tudor women did to their skin to create their 'perfect face'.

The modern cosmetics industry is big business: shops and the media offer us thousands of products to make us look more beautiful, healthier, younger and more attractive. It wasn't like this in Tudor times but rich women in particular wanted to look their best. Many women made their own cosmetics, often with disastrous effects.

To be considered beautiful and wealthy, a Tudor woman desired pure white skin, ruby red lips, rosy cheeks, bright eyes and fair hair. A rich woman wanted white skin because she didn't want anyone to think that she needed to spend any time outside working and getting a tanned face.

Tudor women did many things to their faces to gain the 'perfect face'.

Today, many women (and men) suffer to make themselves look good. However, all our modern day suffering doesn't compare to the pain a Tudor woman must have gone through. She really was a fashion victim.

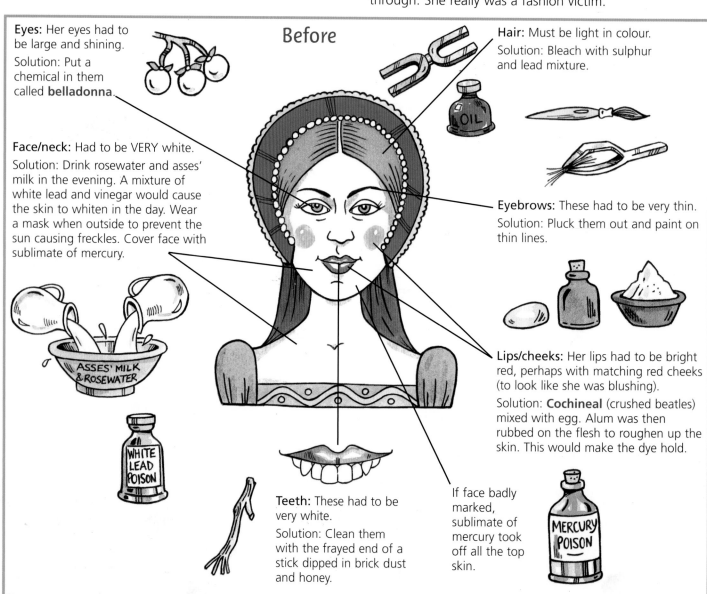

Before

Eyes: Her eyes had to be large and shining.
Solution: Put a chemical in them called **belladonna**.

Face/neck: Had to be VERY white.
Solution: Drink rosewater and asses' milk in the evening. A mixture of white lead and vinegar would cause the skin to whiten in the day. Wear a mask when outside to prevent the sun causing freckles. Cover face with sublimate of mercury.

Hair: Must be light in colour.
Solution: Bleach with sulphur and lead mixture.

Eyebrows: These had to be very thin.
Solution: Pluck them out and paint on thin lines.

Lips/cheeks: Her lips had to be bright red, perhaps with matching red cheeks (to look like she was blushing).
Solution: **Cochineal** (crushed beatles) mixed with egg. Alum was then rubbed on the flesh to roughen up the skin. This would make the dye hold.

Teeth: These had to be very white.
Solution: Clean them with the frayed end of a stick dipped in brick dust and honey.

If face badly marked, sublimate of mercury took off all the top skin.

ASSES' MILK & ROSEWATER

WHITE LEAD POISON

MERCURY POISON

OIL

After

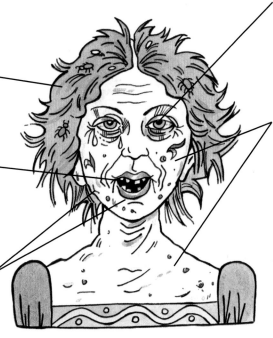

Hair: Women would use sulphur and lead to try to bleach their hair as light as possible. However, this would cause a woman's hair to fall out. Until that happened, she would pile her hair on top of her head. It would have been full of lice and other vermin because she rarely washed it.

Teeth: Most women over the age of 20 had smelly mouths, full of black teeth. As well as removing stains, the brick dust removed the enamel on the teeth leaving them prone to decay.

Lips/cheeks: Cochineal was one of the safest substances used (we still use it today in cake icing – enjoy!). Alum, however, caused their skin to become very rough and scarred.

Eyes: Belladonna was made from deadly nightshade that was extremely poisonous and damaged the eyes of the user. It fogged their vision so they couldn't see properly.

Face/neck: White lead was extremely poisonous. It caused women to have wrinkles and, even worse, open sores that didn't heal. Sublimate of mercury is a very nasty chemical. It caused women's skin to peel like flaking paint. They hoped that the new layer of skin underneath, which would have been very painful to touch, would be whiter than the last.

! FACT Bath time

The Tudors thought bathing was unhealthy and very rarely washed. Even Queen Elizabeth, who was regarded as being extremely clean, only bathed two or three times per year. No wonder people carried scented items around with them and wore lots of expensive perfume, **imported** from the East – what a stink!

★ WISE-UP Words

belladonna
cochineal
imported

Work

1 a Listed below are some chemicals that Tudor women used. Write them out in your book. Next to each one, write down what each was used for. For example: Belladonna – a chemical made from deadly nightshade, used to make Tudor women's eyes shine.

belladonna • cochineal • white lead • brick dust • sulphur • mercury

b Now write down the effects, if any, on a Tudor woman's face.

2 Why did a rich Tudor woman want white skin?

3 a Using a full page in your book, draw an outline of a Tudor woman's face. Around the face, make a brief note of your favourite five Tudor beauty tips. Add the title 'My top five Tudor beauty tips'.

b Using another full page, draw an outline of your face. Around your face, make notes of your own beauty tips (don't be shy, we all try to look after our hair, face and teeth). Add the title 'My own top five beauty tips'.

c What are the main differences between the way we look after our faces and the way they did in Tudor times? Think carefully – are there any similarities?

✚ Hungry for MORE

Imagine you were an older Tudor woman whose face had suffered after years of damage from her strict 'beauty' regime. Design a warning leaflet to hand out to younger girls, outlining the dangers of all the terrible treatments.

___MISSION ACCOMPLISHED?___

- Can you name three chemicals used by Tudor women in an attempt to improve their looks?
- Can you outline the damage these chemicals did?

A day in the life

MISSION OBJECTIVES

• To understand how and why our modern daily routine differs from those of people in Tudor England.

Most of us get up around the same time – probably between 6:30–8:00am. We eat lunch and dinner at similar times and probably go to bed around the same time as well. We tend to call this our routine – a well established pattern of behaviour we follow almost all the time.

There are other things in our lives that most of us do too. We eat similar things, drink similar things and even get our food from similar places. So what routines did people follow in Tudor England? Did daily life differ between rich and poor? And how did things change after the Tudors?

In Tudor times, the average country worker got up at dawn and worked until 4:00 or 5:00 in the afternoon. At busy times of the year, such as harvest time, work would go on later, with men, women and children working out in the fields until it was too dark to see. Workers would stop a couple of times each day for a break – eating a breakfast of bread and ale at 7:00am and a lunch of bread, cheese and ale around 11:00am.

The main meal of the day was eaten around 6:00pm when the workers came in from the fields. They usually ate a kind of stew (called pottage) which was almost entirely made up of vegetables such as turnips, cabbages, parsnips, onions, carrots, and peas. They had bread (again) with this because the poor ate very little meat. Sometimes they caught rabbits or fish, or had a breast of chicken or bacon, but it was only the rich who could afford to buy (or hunt) for meat.

The rich got up early too, between 5–6:00am, and ate breakfast around 7:00am. Like the ordinary country workers, breakfast would consist of bread and beer but a rich family's breakfast table might include meat or fish too.

Dinner time was also around 12 o'clock and consisted of lots of courses, served one after the other. Beef, pork, mutton and fish would be offered but more unusual foods such as roasted pigeon, seagulls, lobster and peacock might appear as well. Salads and fruit pies were common, all washed down with beer, wine, sherry (or 'sack') and cider. Food was eaten with a spoon and a sharp pointed knife but by 1620 some people had started to use forks – some with eight prongs!

! FACT What time is it?

The name we give to 12 o'clock is 'midday', a shorter version of 'Middle of the day'. But have you ever thought that 12 o'clock midday is not really the middle of the day in today's world at all? Nowadays, most adults get up around 7:00am (five hours before midday) and go to bed at 11:00pm (eleven hours after midday). In fact, the real middle of the day for most people today is around 3:00pm.

! FACT A rotten tale

Most food was heavily salted or smoked, to stop it rotting (no refrigerators you see!). Flavourings such as garlic, cinnamon, cloves and vinegar were used to disguise the salty taste.

'The first course at dinner pottage or stew boiled meat or stewed meat. Chicken and bacon, powdered beef [chopped up finely] pies, goose, pig, roasted beef, roasted veal, custard. The second course at dinner: roasted lamb, roasted capons [chickens], roasted conies [rabbits], chickens, peahens, baked venison, tart'

↰ **SOURCE A:** *A menu from 1580 for a well-off family. NOTE: that there is no mention of vegetables.*

WISE-UP Words

routine

Key

1 Stone paving slabs covered the floor – rushes were scattered over them to make it more comfortable.

2 Plastered walls but over one of them is a large painted cloth or tapestry.

3 Trestle table covered in table cloth.

4 Two carved chairs for mother and father – sometimes cushions were added for comfort.

5 Stools or benches for the children.

6 Oak chest sometimes containing valuable family items like silver candlesticks or gold plates.

7 Some of the plates were made from thick pottery or pewter. Pewter is made from tin and lead. In richer families the plates might be made from silver.

8 Spoons and knives were used but diners still ate much of their food with their fingers. Forks were rarely used until the mid 1600s.

9 A rushlight, made from rushes soaked in grease. It burned very slowly.

10 Ale was the main drink. Drinking glasses began to appear in the 16th century, usually imported from Italy.

11 - Hot meat pies

12 - Cheese

13 - Pickled herrings

14 - Roast pigeon

15 - Roast beef

16 - Apple pie

17 - Leg of mutton

18 - Bread

19 - Fish plate containing pike, eels, salmon and carp

↰ **SOURCE B:** *A wealthy Tudor family enjoying their dinner.*

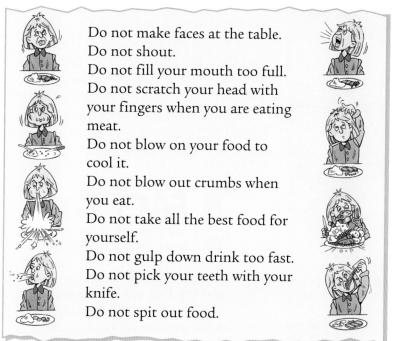

Do not make faces at the table.
Do not shout.
Do not fill your mouth too full.
Do not scratch your head with your fingers when you are eating meat.
Do not blow on your food to cool it.
Do not blow out crumbs when you eat.
Do not take all the best food for yourself.
Do not gulp down drink too fast.
Do not pick your teeth with your knife.
Do not spit out food.

↰ **SOURCE C:** *Tudor table manners. These 'top tips' for table behaviour appeared in a Tudor book in 1577. Amazingly, most of us will have learned some of these tips when we were young!*

❗ FACT Fancy a brew

In the early 1600s, the three most common hot drinks, tea, coffee and cocoa, were introduced. Cocoa from Mexico, coffee from Arabia and tea from China.

24 cows
100 fat sheep
51 great veals
100 pigs
700 chickens
444 pigeons
168 swans
4000 larks

↳ **SOURCE D:** *A list of food eaten by Henry VIII and his guests during November 1531. Rich Tudors were fond of creating amusing food to eat. For example, they would sew the front end of a chicken to the back end of a pig before cooking it. They would also, quite literally bake four and twenty blackbirds in a pie.*

___**MISSION ACCOMPLISHED?**___

• Can you identify three key differences, in both routine and foods eaten, between daily life today and the lives of those people in Tudor England?

59

ENGLAND ABROAD

People in Medieval England led very simple lives. They ate food that they had grown or slaughtered themselves and drank ale they brewed at home. The simple furniture they owned would be made by the village carpenter and any metal items they needed were knocked up by the village blacksmith. All that changed in the Tudor period. Overall, people were better off and they wanted to spend their money on exotic luxuries from far-away lands. People soon realised that they could get rich by fetching these foreign goods for an eager English public and trading companies were set up. But what were these products? Where in the world did they come from? And how did this trade lead to England having an Empire?

1: How did Britain build an Empire?

MISSION OBJECTIVES

- To know how and why England started to trade with countries all over the world.
- To understand how this trade led to England having an Empire.

In the Company of kings and queens

Rich people worked out that if they could buy popular items abroad – where they were cheap – and bring them back to England – where they would sell for high prices – they could make a fortune. A number of rich businessmen formed groups – or companies – and asked Queen Elizabeth, and later James I, for permission to trade with different parts of the world.

Today, large businesses trade with countries all over the world. Things were very different under the Tudors as each company kept to its own area. The most successful and most famous was the East India Company, which was founded in 1600 by a group of London businessmen. Their money paid for ships and crews to sail around the south of Africa to India. Once they had reached India, English goods such as fine woolen cloth and silver were traded for the things that Europeans were desperate for – spices, silk, ivory and precious stones.

The Moscow Company

The Virginia Company

TAR

COTTON

The Turkey Company

The East India Company

The Venetian Company

! FACT Spice up your life

We may not think of spices as expensive or precious goods these days, but it wasn't always that way. Simple pepper was the East India Company's biggest earner and nutmeg – which people believed cured the plague – could be sold for a 600 000% profit!

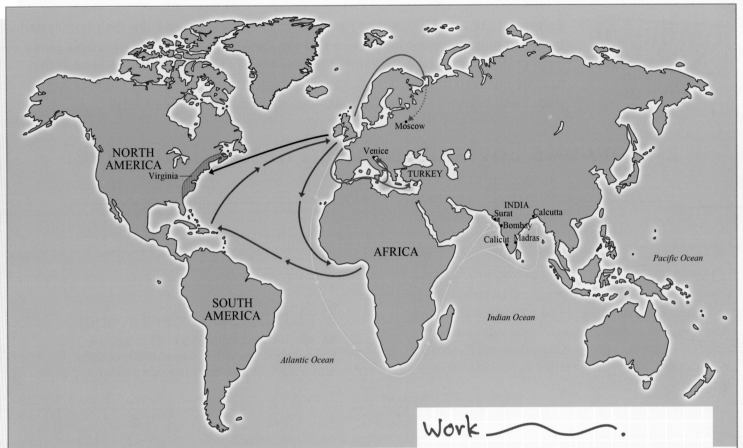

British ships travelled all over the world in search of goods to sell back home – and huge profits.

From Trade to Empire

It wasn't just English people who realised that huge profits could be made by trading abroad. France, Spain, Holland and Portugal all had trading companies that were in fierce competition with both English traders and each other. This led to companies trying to gain complete control of areas they traded in by creating colonies. In North America, most of the east coast was claimed by England in 1607. More settlers arrived from England, attracted by the huge profits made by growing and selling tobacco. A Dutch colony called New Amsterdam was taken over and re-named New York. By 1750, the East coast of America was under British control. In India, the East India Company paid the local rulers to allow them to set up trading stations at Surat, Bombay (now Mumbai), Calicut, Madras and Calcutta. The company had its own private army and, from these bases, gradually increased its power until all of India was under British rule.

⭫ **SOURCE A:**
The East India Company's sale catalogue for March 1704.

Work

Copy out these headings in your book:

Moscow Co. • Venitian Co. • East India Co. • Virginia Co. • Turkey Co.

1 Write the following products under the name of the company that bought and sold them.
Spices, jewels, carpets, cotton, wine, sugar, silks, tar, rope, timber, spices, furs, carpets, Tobacco, olive oil, currants.

2 a Why did trading in foreign goods lead to England controlling other countries? Answer in full sentences using capital letters and full stops.

b What evidence is there in the place names that English people settled in North America?

3 Imagine you are a wealthy Tudor gentleman from London. Write a letter to a friend and try to persuade him to join the East India Company. Explain what they would buy with his money, what goods would be brought back from India and how he would make a huge profit.

——— **MISSION ACCOMPLISHED?**———

• Can you name three countries with which England traded?

• Could you name three products from abroad that became popular in England?

• Can you tell somebody how trading led to England owning parts of other countries?

Between 1518 and 1800, over 11 million Africans were taken from their homes and forced to become slaves in America and the Caribbean. Thousands of people made huge profits out of the enslavement of millions of African people. The English first became involved in 1562. So where were these slaves taken? How did they get there? And how did Englishmen make money from this terrible trade?

2: How was England involved in the slave trade?

MISSION OBJECTIVES

- To understand what the word 'slave' means.
- To be able to explain how the transatlantic slave triangle worked and how it started.

A ship would leave England loaded with manufactured goods. In Africa, the English goods would be exchanged. The slaves would be loaded onto the ships and taken on a horrific journey to the West Indies, or North or South America. It was said at the time that conditions on board were so bad you could smell a slave ship about 10km away.

After selling the slaves, the shipowner would load his ship again but this time with cotton, sugar or tobacco, and sail back to England. These goods were very popular (and expensive) in Europe and could be sold for a small fortune. Everyone profited from the slave trade… except the slaves!

John Hawkins was the first Englishman to ship slaves to America. Farming tobacco, cotton and sugar was hard work and the European farmers didn't want to do it. They were more than willing to pay £60 for a slave to do it.

European traders were willing to sell slaves. By 1564, Hawkins was making so much money that he asked Queen Elizabeth to alter his family's coat of arms to include his new money making scheme. Look carefully at Source B to see his new coat of arms.

▋▋ PAUSE for Thought
Before beginning with this page, think about the word 'slave'. Who or what was a slave? What does the word mean?

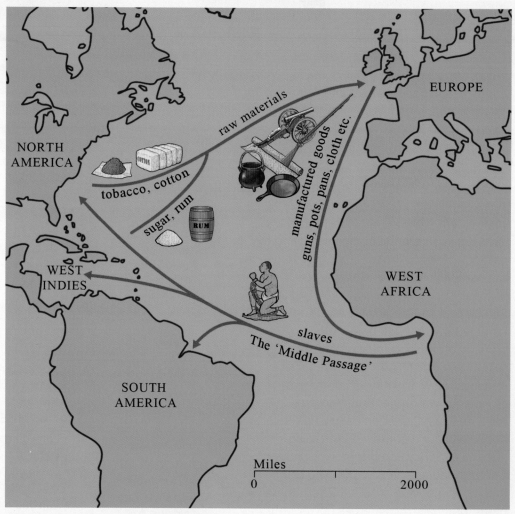

The slave trade was often called the 'slave triangle'.

Official figures show that between 1690 and 1787, over 11 000 English ships took slaves to the West Indies and America. Many Englishmen played a significant part in the slave trade – shipowners, slave traders, and cotton, sugar and tobacco **importers**. But the slave trade also provided work for dockworkers unloading ships, factory workers turning the slave cotton into shirts, and shopowners selling sugar and tobacco. Many thousands of English people made money out of the trade in human beings.

WISE-UP Words

enslavement
importers
slave

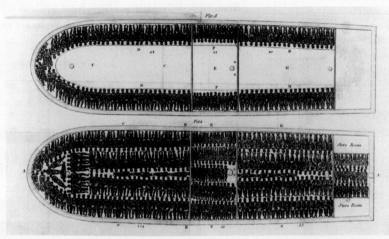

⬑ **SOURCE A:** *Hundreds of slaves were packed onto the cramped ships and chained together. There were no toilets and hardly any food. Why do you think diseases spread easily?*

⬑ **SOURCE B:** *John Hawkins' coat of arms.*

To be sold:
James – A pretty little negro boy, about nine years old, and well limbed. A good worker.
Toby – A strong boy, about 15, intelligent, a good driver and knows about coffee.
Ben – Past his prime with a bad arm.
To be seen at the Dolphin Tavern.

⬑ **SOURCE C:** *From about 1570, a few Africans were bought to work in England. This advert is from a London newspaper. Similar sales happened in ports such as Liverpool and Bristol.*

Work

1 Explain your ideas about what the word 'slave' means.

2 a Copy the diagram of the 'slave triangle'. Why was it so profitable for a shipowner?

b Write three sentences about conditions on board a slave ship. Use Source A to help you.

3 Look closely at Source B. How can you tell that John Hawkins was involved with the slave trade?

4 Look at Source C.

a Which slave do you think would fetch the best price? Why?

b Which slave do you think would fetch the lowest price? Why?

5 Today, we think the idea of slavery is wrong, although trade in human lives – people trafficking – does go on. John Hawkins and many like him saw nothing wrong with the selling of slaves. Why do you think opinions have changed so much?

➕ **Hungry for MORE**
The slave trade didn't last forever. Try to find out details about the end of slavery.
• When did it end?
• Why did it end?
• Who was responsible for helping to end slavery?

—— **MISSION ACCOMPLISHED?** ——
• Could you tell somebody what a slave is?
• Can you name three things that were traded in the transatlantic slave trade other than people?
• Do you know how people made money from this trade triangle?

63

On 12 April 1600, a battered and leaking ship sailed into an unknown port. It had been at sea for 19 months, the sails were ripped to shreds, food had run out long ago and only 24 of the 100 crew members were left alive. One of those still breathing was an Englishman called William Adams. He had survived Antarctic blizzards, tropical storms and eaten rats when the supplies ran out. When he checked the charts to see where he was, he saw only squiggles, question marks and sea monsters. They had sailed off the edge of the map! So what was this strange new land they had arrived in? What kind of people lived there? And would they be welcomed?

3: Samurai Bill – the first Englishman in Japan

MISSION OBJECTIVES

- To know how life in Japan was different from life in England in 1600.
- To know what was special about the life of William Adams.

Japan – the land on the edge of the world.

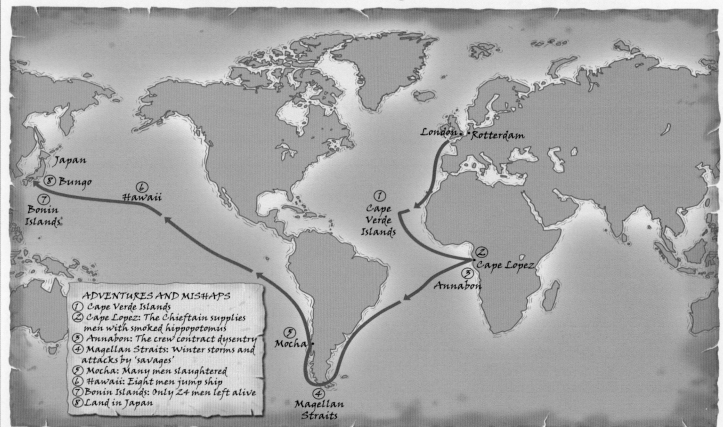

ADVENTURES AND MISHAPS
1. Cape Verde Islands
2. Cape Lopez: The Chieftain supplies men with smoked hippopotomus
3. Annabon: The crew contract dysentry
4. Magellan Straits: Winter storms and attacks by 'savages'
5. Mocha: Many men slaughtered
6. Hawaii: Eight men jump ship
7. Bonin Islands: Only 24 men left alive
8. Land in Japan

Adams and his shipmates (who were all Dutch) had washed up in the land of Japan. They had no idea how the men who were rowing out to meet them would treat them. They had heard stories of 'wilde men', savages and cannibals. What they saw shocked them but not in the way they expected! What amazed them was how advanced the Japanese were, with customs, cities and standards of cleanliness that left the Europeans feeling like they were the savages.

'This strange-looking race wore their hair plucked at the front but tied into a large bun at the back. They wore exquisite silk robes with terrifying curved swords that could slice through bone.'

↳ SOURCE A: Extract from the book 'Samurai William – the adventurer who unlocked Japan'.

↳ **SOURCE B:** *The best Japanese warriors were known as Samurai. Adams described them as 'valiant' but they never took prisoners and would rather commit suicide than be captured.*

The life of William Adams

Far from being killed, Adams became a firm favourite of the Japanese ruler, Ieyasu. Adams soon learned to speak Japanese and taught Ieyasu mathematics and the methods he had used to sail the huge distances to Japan.

He was given the title of Hatamoto – a kind of baron – and lived the rest of his days as a Japanese nobleman. The locals called him Anjim Sama – which means Mr Pilot. An area of of Tokyo was even named in his honour – Anjincho!

Work

1 William Adams soon found that the Japanese had different approaches to lots of things. Read through the sources and write a sentence describing the Japanese attitudes to:

food • hygiene • eating • war • personal hygiene • medicine

2 Imagine you are a Japanese villager who witnessed William Adams and his shipmates coming ashore. Write a letter to a friend explaining what the Europeans look like, how they act and the impression they have made on you.

3 Write an obituary for William Adams to appear in the *London Times* newspaper. Make sure you include as much detail about the life and achievements of the first Englishman in Japan as you can.

'They so imitate the Japanese, that they wear their clothes, speak their language and eat like them on the floor... they eat with small sticks, observing the same ceremonies as the Japanese do themselves.'

↳ **SOURCE C:** *The views of a shocked Portuguese monk when he first saw how his fellow countrymen behaved in Japan.*

'All of the noble houses have bathrooms for guests that are provided with hot water. It is the custom in Japan to wash at least twice a day.'

↳ **SOURCE D:** *Observations of a Portugese visitor. Europeans did not wash at sea and their appearance shocked the Japanese.*

'They are astonished by eating with hands... it causes disgust. All of the food is cut up on spotless tables with iron knives and nothing is touched by the hands.'

↳ **SOURCE E:** *What the same visitor said about eating and preparing food.*

'The Japanese would rather die than use our surgical remedies. In all their sicknesses, they have their stomach, arms and back etc. pierced with silver needles.'

↳ **SOURCE F:** *Extract from the book 'Samurai William – the adventurer who unlocked Japan'.*

MISSION ACCOMPLISHED?

• Could you name two ways in which Japan was more advanced than England in the early seventeenth century?

• Do you know what the Japanese thought of their European visitors?

• Could you tell somebody about the key events in William Adam's life?

Blackbeard is the most famous of all pirates. His ship, the *Queen Anne's revenge*, which he captured from the French, terrorized the seas from 1716–1718. Born in Bristol in 1680, Blackbeard's real name was Edward Drummand. He was a huge man who realised that one of his main weapons was terror. It wasn't long before he had a terrifying reputation. So could you handle life at sea with Blackbeard the blood-thirsty pirate?

4: Blackbeard – the original pirate of the Caribbean

MISSION OBJECTIVES

- To know who Blackbeard was and why was he so terrifying.
- To be able to explain the difference between a pirate and a privateer.

Blackbeard loved the pirate life. However, he had once been a privateer, working for the Queen of England, Anne. Privateers had special permission to rob any foreign ships of any gold, silver, sugar, rum, cotton, cocoa or any other valuable goods. Many European nations were bringing these back from the 'New World' of North and South America and privateers saw their chance to make money.

He stuck slow-burning matches into his hair and beard. Smoke curled around his face.

Long black hair.

Big, bushy black beard.

He carried six pistols in a belt strung over his hairy chest.

Two swords and several daggers.

Blackbeard's ship, Queen Anne's Revenge. *At any one time there were 120–150 pirates on board.*

Anything a privateer stole would be shared with the monarch… but Blackbeard hated sharing, so he became a pirate instead. Pirates would rob anybody, even ships from their own country. This made pirates very rich – but they ran the risk of becoming hunted men by their own nation.

⌐ SOURCE A: *Blackbeard's pirate flag.*

Injury	Payment
Loss of both legs	1500 pieces of eight or 15 slaves
Loss of both hands	1800 pieces of eight or 18 slaves
For one leg	600 pieces of eight or 6 slaves
For one hand	same as a leg
Loss of an eye	100 pieces of eight or 1 slave

⌐ SOURCE C: *An agreement drawn up by pirates in case of injury.*

Being a member of Blackbeard's pirate crew was a risky business too. Conditions on board ship were terrible – rats, fleas, mice, lice – and keeping food fresh was a constant problem. The pirates tended to live on salted beef or pork, fish, biscuits and beer. Often their food went rotten, so they longed to capture a ship full of good things to eat.

'Blackbeard would kill a member of his crew now and then, just to remind the others who was boss. One captured crew member said "if he did not now and then kill one of them, they would forget who he was".'

⌐ SOURCE B: *A modern historian.*

Blackbeard's reign didn't last forever. Lieutenant Robert Maynard of the English Royal Navy was given the job of tracking him down. He spotted Blackbeard's ship on 22 November 1718. After a fierce ship battle in which Blackbeard was shot (five times), stabbed (20 times) and slashed across the throat, he was killed whilst trying to load his gun. And because it was a custom of the time to display dead pirates as a warning to others, Maynard cut off Blackbeard's head and hung it up on the front of his ship until it rotted. The remaining crew members were hanged.

According to legend, Blackbeard's skull was made into a cup soon after his death. Today there is a huge reward for anyone who can find it.

Work

1 In your own words, explain the difference between a pirate and a privateer?

2 Here are some key events in Blackbeard's life – but they are all mixed up! Write them out in the order in which they happened:
- captured the *Queen Anne's Revenge*;
- was shot, stabbed and slashed across the throat;
- became a pirate;
- born in Bristol in 1680;
- Robert Maynard given job of hunting him down;
- head displayed on Maynard's ship;
- worked as a privateer for Queen Anne.

3 It is 1718. Imagine you were one of Blackbeard's pirate crew and have just been captured by Robert Maynard. It has been discovered that you have kept a diary over the last few years. Write at least three diary entries that gave details of your pirate life over the past few years. Remember to include:
- Information about your boss, Blackbeard: What does he look like? Has he always been a pirate? How tough is he?
- Facts about the life of a pirate – What are conditions on board a ship like? What do you eat? Is it dangerous? How successful was Blackbeard's crew?
- Details about the hunt for Blackbeard – Who hunted him? How was Blackbeard killed? What happened to his body? What might happen to you?

—— MISSION ACCOMPLISHED?——
- Can you explain the difference between a pirate and a privateer?

Young Elizabeth – what was she like?

MISSION OBJECTIVES

- To understand why Princess Elizabeth, King Henry VIII's youngest daughter, was such a clever student.
- To understand the circumstances in which she became queen.

In 1533, King Henry's second wife, Anne Boleyn, announced she was pregnant. The King desperately wanted a son who could be king after him. He already had one daughter, Mary, and he didn't want another one. He worried that a woman would never be clever or strong enough to run a country.

On the 7 September 1533, Princess Elizabeth Tudor was born. Henry was very disappointed. He sulked for weeks and didn't even attend her christening! Elizabeth was two years old when her mum was executed and over the next few years she would have four different step-mothers. Elizabeth never lived with her dad and was sent to live with her half-sister, Mary.

The girls had three houses: Hatfield and Eltham near London and Thursdon in Hertfordshire. When they travelled between each house, they would fight over who would walk at the front of the procession. It doesn't appear to have been an easy life for young Elizabeth: a dead mother, a tough father, an awkward half-sister and lots of step-mothers. And when her brother Edward was born, it didn't look like she would ever be queen!

But despite some difficulties in her life, Princess Elizabeth had one major factor in her favour – she was bright and clever. In fact, by the time she was 16, she could speak five languages – English, French, Italian, Greek and Latin. So what was the secret of her success? Study the cartoons and the sources carefully – they outline why Lizzy was such a clever young lady!

SECRET OF HER SUCCESS NO. 1: she enjoyed learning.

Elizabeth had her own personal tutors and seemed to really enjoy working hard at her lessons. It was very fashionable at the time for rich young women to be highly educated and Lizzy seemed to love writing poems, translating foreign books and learning new languages.

SECRET OF HER SUCCESS NO. 2: she got attention because she was clever.

King Henry was disappointed when Elizabeth was born but soon grew to love spending time with his clever daughter. When Henry visited Elizabeth, her half-sister was probably very jealous – Mary was locked away in a separate room whilst the King and his youngest daughter chatted, swapped gifts and sang together.

SECRET OF HER SUCCESS NO. 3: she was lonely.

Elizabeth didn't really have any real friends, mainly due to the fact that most of the people she knew were working for her – tutors, cooks, maids, musicians and so on. But reading books and learning new skills meant that she could talk about them with people. People weren't going to voice their real opinions about England to the King's daughter but they might be honest about their views on books, music and horses.

SECRET OF HER SUCCESS NO. 4: there wasn't much else to do.

There was no television, radio, Internet or computer games in Tudor England. Books, music and horse riding provided entertainment for her – and she seemed to be very good at many of the things she tried.

Monday	Tuesday	Wednesday	Thursday	Friday
Bible Study	Bible Study	Bible Study	Bible Study	Bible Study
Book Translation: Greek to English	Book Translation: English to Greek	Book Translation: Latin to English	Book Translation: English to Latin	Philosophy
	Lunchtime - Food ~ Walking ~ Riding ~ Games			
French Conversation	Italian Conversation	Latin Conversation	English Conversation	Greek Conversation
Philosophy	Book Translation: Latin to English	Book Translation: English to Latin	Book Translation: Greek to English	Book Translation: English to Greek

↰ SOURCE A: *Elizabeth's timetable when she was being taught by one of her tutors.*

'She is most eager. Her mind has no womanly weakness; her perseverance is equal to that of a man and she has a long memory. She talks French and Italian as well as English, and has often talked to me in Latin and Greek. She has beautiful handwriting and is a skilful musician.'

↲ SOURCE B: *Written by one of her tutors, Robert Ascham. Not a bad school report, is it?*

Elizabeth was 13 years old when her father died – and her younger half-brother, Edward, became king (aged nine). Despite being quite close to Edward, many people suspected she might be plotting against him during his short reign (he died aged 15). However, nothing could ever be proved against her.

When her older half-sister, Mary, became queen in 1553, Elizabeth was again suspected of plotting against the monarch – and again nothing could be proved. To be on the safe side, Mary kept Elizabeth almost as a prisoner at various country houses.

Four years later, in 1558, whilst Elizabeth was (typically) sitting reading under a tree at Hatfield House, she received word that Queen Mary was dead, aged 25. Elizabeth was now Queen of England.

↰ SOURCE C: *A painting of Elizabeth aged 13.*

Work

1 What difficulties did Elizabeth face early in her life?

2 Look closely at Source A.

   a Explain why the following subjects take up so much of Elizabeth's study time:
   • Bible study;
   • conversation;
   • learning and translating foreign languages.

   b Think of three subjects that you study at school today that are not on Elizabeth's timetable. Why do you think it is felt important that you study them?

3 Imagine that you are Princess Elizabeth's tutor. King Henry has asked you to write a school report about his daughter. It should include details about:
   • her lessons;
   • her strengths;
   • her attitude towards learning.

   Why don't you set it out like one of your school reports?

MISSION ACCOMPLISHED?

• Can you recall five facts about Princess Elizabeth's early life? For example, can you name all the languages she could speak?

What did Queen Elizabeth look like?

MISSION OBJECTIVES

- To understand why it is so hard to establish what Queen Elizabeth really looked like.
- To understand why Elizabeth controlled her royal portraits so carefully.

Our current monarch is known to millions of people all over the world. Her face is on television, in the newspapers and even on the money we use. Some people have even seen her in real life as she travels around Britain and the world. Her family life has even been made into a soap opera on American television. Many people today are fascinated by our royal family.

In the sixteenth century, ordinary people were also very interested in their queen – Elizabeth I. However, there was no television or daily newspapers to show what she looked like. You might have been lucky enough to glimpse her face as she toured around but it was highly unlikely that an ordinary person would see her for real.

So that her people could know what she looked like, Elizabeth used paintings or portraits. However, Elizabeth was a wise queen and she cleverly controlled pictures that the public saw in order to create an image of herself that would impress everyone. Lord Cecil, who worked for the Queen, once said:

'Many painters have done portraits of the Queen but none has shown her looks and charms. Therefore, she has asked people to stop doing portraits of her until a clever painter has finished one which all other painters can copy. Her Majesty, in the meantime, forbids the showing of any portraits which are ugly, until they are improved.'

SOURCE A ⤸

⤷ SOURCE C

⤷ SOURCE B

The Queen would have official portraits sent to artists to be copied. No other portraits were allowed. For years, the artist would copy these portraits every time an admirer wanted a portrait of the Queen.

Look at the five portraits here (Sources A–E) and see if you can match them to the descriptions (1–5).

SOURCE E

SOURCE D

Important visitors to England who met Elizabeth probably saw a very different person to the lady we see in each of the paintings. Some of the following descriptions are even quite insulting. We must remember that the Queen was over 60 when they were written.

! FACT Smile, please!

Elizabeth sat down to be painted only eight times – but there are over 200 paintings of her that are still in existence today. This shows just how many times artists were instructed to copy other paintings.

Work

1 a Why would it be unlikely that an ordinary person would meet Elizabeth I?

  b Why then, were portraits of the Queen so important for Elizabeth and her subjects?

2 a Select one of the portraits on these pages. In your own words, write a detailed description of Elizabeth from this picture.

  b If Elizabeth herself were to read your description, would she be pleased with what you have written? Explain your answer.

  c Which of the portraits (Sources A–E) do you think Elizabeth would be most pleased with? Explain your answer.

3 Explain why Elizabeth I didn't allow 'the showing of any portraits which are ugly'.

+ Hungry for MORE

Why not draw or paint your own royal portrait? Try basing it on one of the descriptions on this page.

1 Painted in 1588, just after the Spanish had tried, and failed, to invade England. In the background, the artist has painted some wrecked Spanish ships. Elizabeth's hand is on a globe to show she is one of the most powerful people in the world.

2 Painted soon after she was crowned. Elizabeth was about 25 years old. Note the crown, the orb, (the ball) and the sceptre (the long stick), which are symbols of the power and authority of the Queen. Also look at all the jewels and gold-coloured cloth used to show how wealthy she is.

3 An engraving of Elizabeth, created shortly before her death. Notice the 'bags' under her eyes.

4 Painted when she was in her twenties. Look carefully at her dress; it is covered in eyes and ears. What do you think the message is here?

5 Painted when Elizabeth was in her sixties. She is wearing a wig here.

MISSION ACCOMPLISHED?

• Would you be able to write a paragraph explaining how Elizabeth used to control her image and emphasise her power?

There's something about Mary

MISSION OBJECTIVES

- To understand why Mary was heir to England's throne.
- To understand why she became such a threat.
- To understand why she was executed.

By 1568, Elizabeth had been Queen for ten years. She hadn't married and she hadn't any children. This meant that if she died, her cousin, Mary, Queen of Scotland, would become Queen of England and Wales too.

Mary had a troubled past. She was known as a great beauty but had difficulty keeping her husbands! She was married to the King of France – who died in a freak riding accident. She then married an English Lord – who was strangled and blown up. Soon after this, she married the man who was suspected of murdering her second husband!

The Scots were suspicious of Mary's connection to her second husband's death and some rebelled against her. She was forced to give up her throne and stand aside, as her young son, James, was made King of Scotland. In 1568, she ran away to England, perhaps hoping that her cousin, Queen Elizabeth, would take pity on her.

Mary immediately caused problems for Elizabeth. She was Catholic for a start and made no secret of the fact that she thought she should be Queen of England instead of Elizabeth. Some English Catholics even agreed with her. Elizabeth's solution was a harsh but typically clever one. She kept Mary a virtual prisoner until she could make up her mind what to do with her. In fact, Mary was kept in various houses and castles and imprisoned for the next 17 years.

The two women never actually met each other in this time but, finally, Elizabeth was forced to take action against Mary. She had committed the terrible crime of supporting a plan to kill the English Queen!

Babington's plot

In 1586, a young, rich Catholic man called Anthony Babington had a secret plan to kill Elizabeth. He would organise six men to kill the English Queen, rescue Mary from her prison and make her the new Queen of England. However, Babington needed to know if Mary liked the idea. He needed to contact her in prison.

↳ SOURCE A: *This is the part of Mary's letter that led to her execution. Can you work out what she wrote? What does she mean?*

He managed to get Mary's servants to hide secret letters in beer barrels that were taken to her room. The letters were written in code. Mary wrote back saying she agreed to the plan. In fact, Mary's servants didn't work for her at all, they worked for England's chief spy, Sir Francis Walsingham, who took the letters straight to Elizabeth.

When the code was broken, the message was clear: Mary was supporting a plan to kill the Queen. This was **treason**.

Despite all the evidence, Elizabeth still didn't want to have her cousin executed. Eventually, her secretary, Sir John Davidson, slipped the death warrant in among some papers she had to sign. Elizabeth pretended she didn't really know what she was signing, signed it, changed her mind, then tried to stop the execution. But she was too late. Mary Queen of Scots had already been executed.

Work 〜〜.

1 a Why was Mary, Queen of Scotland, next in line to the English throne?

b Explain why Mary ran away from Scotland to England.

2 When Mary arrived in England, Queen Elizabeth had three choices. Should she:
- Send her back to Scotland?
- Put her in prison?
- Allow her to carry on with life in England?

In your own words, write down the choice she made. Then explain why you think she didn't choose the other options.

3 a In your own words, explain how Sir Francis Walsingham arranged to trap Mary.

b Why do you think Elizabeth hesitated over her decision to have Mary executed?

4 Using the code, write out three facts about Mary's life. Make each one short and simple. Pass your coded facts to a friend and see if they can work out what you have written.

WISE-UP Words

treason

___MISSION ACCOMPLISHED?___

- Can you explain who Mary Queen of Scots was, why she was a threat to Queen Elizabeth and why was she executed in 1587?

SOURCE A: *The execution of Mary Queen of Scots in February 1587. The axeman took at least three blows to cut her head off. It was said that her lips continued to move after her head was separated from her body – then her wig fell off!*

Match of the day: England versus Spain

MISSION OBJECTIVES

- To understand why the King of Spain decided to invade England in 1588.
- To identify key reasons why the Spanish Armada failed.

In Tudor times, Spain was the richest, most powerful country in the world. It had a huge army and Spanish treasure ships were bringing a fortune in gold back to Spain from newly discovered lands. But in 1588, Spain's King Philip II decided to focus all his country's great power and wealth on one thing – the invasion of England! He set every shipyard in Spain to work, building what many described as the greatest navy – or Armada – ever created, and this massive fleet of 130 huge warships was heading for one place – England!

So why was Philip so angry with the English? How was his ambitious invasion plan designed to work? And how successful were the Spanish when battle finally commenced in this world famous 'Match of the day'?

Few people had ever seen Philip II, King of Spain, so angry. It was the morning of 20 April 1587 and he had just received some shattering news. The most famous English 'sea dog' of all, Sir Francis Drake, had just sailed into Cadiz harbour in southern Spain and set fire to 30 of Spain's royal warships! Philip was furious but had other reasons to be mad with the English:

- For years, the English sailors had been stealing gold and silver from Spanish ships.
- Philip (a Catholic) had recently heard news that Mary Queen of Scots (another Catholic) had been executed by Elizabeth I. He thought that the people who had killed a Catholic queen should be punished.
- Philip was fighting to keep the Spanish Netherlands (now known as Holland and Belgium) under his control. However, the Dutch rebels were being helped by soldiers from another country – yes, you've guessed it… England!

By the summer of 1588, Philip's forces had recovered from Drake's attack on Cadiz and he had assembled one of the greatest fleets of warships the world had ever seen. There were 130 Spanish ships, known as an **Armada**, many painted red and gold, which together covered an area of about 12km of sea. His aim for the fleet was simple – meet up with 20 000 ground troops at Calais, transport them to invade England and remove Elizabeth from the English throne. He would then turn Protestant England into a Catholic country once more.

NEXT FIXTURE

The English Navy
Owner: Queen Elizabeth

Managers: Sir Francis Drake and Lord Howard

Vs

The Spanish Armada
Owner: King Philip II

Manager: The Duke of Medina Sidonia

Date: Summer 1588
Venue: The English Channel

The Spanish have a fantastic fleet and they're confident that they will beat the English. They even call themselves the 'invincible Armada'. They do have a problem though. Their commander, the Duke of Medina Sidonia, suffers from seasickness. Can you believe that? A seasick sea captain!

⤒ SOURCE A: *The Armada.*

WISE-UP Words

Armada
galleon   muskets

Work

1 a Why did Philip decide to attack England in 1588?

b What was his plan if his invasion was a success?

2 a In your own words, describe how an English or a Spanish ship's captain would try to defeat an enemy. You might wish to illustrate your answer.

b In your opinion, which fleet of ships, the English or the Spanish, stood the best chance of success? Explain your answer carefully.

ENGLAND

An English galleon

NO. OF SHIPS: 75%

LENGTH OF SHIPS: 50%

MOBILITY: 70%

NO. OF SAILORS: 80%

WEAPONS: 90%

ABILITY OF COMMANDERS: 85%

The English are 'speedy smashers'. Their experienced sailors should be able to avoid any enemy attempts to get alongside. Instead, they will hope to position their ships 150m away and use their superior guns to first fire huge solid 20kg cannonballs through the side of the enemy ships. Then the smaller cannons known as 'man killers' will fire 8kg balls at the sailors. When the Spanish ships are floating wrecks packed with battered and tired soldiers, the English will hop on board and finish them off.

SPAIN

A Spanish galleon

NO. OF SHIPS: 75%

LENGTH OF SHIPS: 90%

MOBILITY: 40%

NO. OF SAILORS: 85%

WEAPONS: 60%

ABILITY OF COMMANDERS: 35%

The Spanish are 'ropers and raiders'. Their ships are like huge floating castles, but are clumsy to steer. So the Spanish **galleons** will try to sail alongside the enemy ships and tie themselves alongside with ropes and hooks. Then soldiers will jump onto the enemy ships and fight with swords, daggers and **muskets**. The heavy guns below decks will almost touch the other ships, and will blow holes in their sides.

The English can field a strong team – about 130 ships, but only 60 or so are fit to fight. The Spanish galleons are about 50 metres long, but the English ones are about half that length. As a result the English ships are much quicker. They have two other advantages: firstly, they pack some of the most accurate long-range guns ever built, and secondly, most of them use the same standard size cannonball. Spanish ships have guns of different sizes and types, and finding the right size of cannonball for each gun during the heat of battle must be tricky!

King Philip's plan was an ambitious one. His fleet of 170 ships would sail up the English Channel to Calais and pick up Spanish soldiers waiting there for them. The force of 30 000 soldiers and sailors would cross the Channel, capture London and replace Queen Elizabeth with a Catholic monarch.

The Armada left Spain on 2 July 1588. They were immediately spotted by a fast sailing boat heading for England. News that the Spanish were on their way would reach England long before they arrived – the English would know they were coming.

1 170 ships set out, sailing packed together in a **crescent** shape, which the English would find difficult to attack.

2 The Spanish are spotted off Cornwall on 29 July and **beacons** are lit on hilltops to warn people of a possible invasion. The English Navy chases the Spaniards for over one week but cannot sink a single Spanish ship.

3 The Spanish arrive in Calais on 5 August. They wait for soldiers to join them but the soldiers do not arrive!

4 Sir Francis Drake attacks the Spanish ships with a weapon they fear the most – FIRESHIPS. Eight old ships are filled with straw, gunpowder, tar and barrels of pig fat and then set alight. They act like floating bombs and drift towards the Spanish, who panic when they see them.

5 Frightened by the fireships, the Spanish scatter in ones and twos, all over the North Sea. The fast English ships attack again and again.

The failure of the Spanish Armada proved that Spain was beatable. Spanish kings could no longer do as they wished and perhaps they began to think that God wasn't on their side.

On the other hand, Elizabeth believed her island was safe from attack but would always need a strong navy to protect it. She began to build up a navy and soon it would begin to venture out in search of valuable new land all over the world.

> 'My health is not equal to this voyage. I know from my experiences at sea that I am always seasick and always catch a cold.'

↰ **SOURCE B:** *The commander of Spain's Armada was the Duke of Medina Sidonia. He was good at paperwork but had no experience of the sea or war, and he suffered from seasickness.*

6 The Spaniards flee. A sudden storm batters their ships as they struggle home around Scotland and Ireland.

7 Nearly every Spanish ship is damaged. The sailors starve as their food goes mouldy. Injured men die when their wounds become infected. As ships sink, some sailors manage to stagger ashore, only to be attacked by the Scottish and Irish.

WISE-UP Words

beacon
crescent

! FACT Famous speeches

Some of the most famous lines in British history were spoken during the time of the Spanish Armada. Legend has it that Sir Francis Drake, Vice Admiral of the English Navy, was playing bowls when he was told that the Spanish had been seen near England's shores. He calmly replied, 'We have enough time to finish the game and beat the Spaniards too.'

Queen Elizabeth visited her troops on 18 August. Dressed in white and silver and riding a white horse, she said, 'I know I have the body of a weak and feeble woman, but I have the heart and stomach of a king, and a king of England too, and think foul scorn that… Spain… should dare invade the border of my realm.'

Work

1 Sketch a map of the route taken by the Spanish Armada in 1588. Label your map with brief sentences, highlighting the most important events of the Armada's journey.

2 The following are all reasons why the Spanish Armada failed:
  • bad weather;
  • fireships;
  • faster English ships;
  • the good leadership of the English;
  • the delay of the Spanish soldiers at Calais.

  a Can you think of any others?

  b List the reasons for the Spanish failure in your book. Start with the most important first, going to the least important last.

  c Explain the reasons for your order.

3 Reread the speeches made by Francis Drake and Queen Elizabeth I and answer the following questions:

  a What do you think both Drake and Elizabeth hoped people would feel when they heard their words?

  b Why do you think we still remember those famous words today?

4 Design your own Armada medal to celebrate victory over the Spanish.

___MISSION ACCOMPLISHED? ___

• Can you identify three key reasons why the Spanish Armada failed?

The scruffy Stuart!

MISSION OBJECTIVES

- To understand why the throne of England passed to the Scottish Royal family.
- To know what England's new Scottish king believed about the nature of kingship.

On a cold, wet day in early 1603, Queen Elizabeth went out for a ten-mile horse ride. The next day, she went out for a long walk, before staying up all night dancing and talking. It was an amazing thing for a 69-year-old woman to do. By the end of the week, she was seriously ill with pneumonia. She had throat ulcers and terrible chest pains but still refused to rest properly. On 15 March, she stood upright for 15 hours to show everyone that she was still strong. But not even Elizabeth, with all her strength and determination, could live forever. Soon she couldn't speak, eat or move about. She spent her days and nights lying on a huge pile of cushions staring at a fire.

Despite being queen for 45 years, Elizabeth had never married or had any children. This worried her advisors – who would rule after she died? Elizabeth had never said who she wanted to replace her. Perhaps she didn't want to think about dying! Now, in the Queen's final days, her advisors named Elizabeth's cousin, James VI of Scotland, as her successor. She nodded and raised her hand to show that she agreed.

In the early hours of the next morning, on the 23 March 1603, she died. A messenger called Robert Carey jumped on the first of a string of fast horses and galloped up to Scotland to tell James. James VI, King of Scotland, also became James I of England. One man with two countries to rule. Sixty hours later, dirty, tired and injured after a fall on the way, the 37-year-old king arrived in London. The crowds that cheered him were witnessing one of the most famous royal family changes in English history. The Tudor period had ended and now a new Scottish family, the Stuarts, had arrived to rule England.

FACT FILE: James I 'the scruffy Stuart'

Name: James Stuart, the late Queen Elizabeth's cousin.

Age: 37

Job title: King James I of England and King James VI of Scotland.

Early career: He was a very successful King of Scotland. He managed to control both rich and powerful lords and highland chiefs whenever they showed any sign of rebellion. He divided Scotland into four districts and appointed Royal judges to visit each area twice a year to hold criminal trials. He invited weavers from abroad to teach Scottish clothmakers how to make better cloth that could be sold abroad and encouraged gold, silver and coal mining. King James even managed to keep control of the Scottish (Protestant) church!

Intelligence: A clever chap who wrote several books. His favourite subject was witchcraft. He also wrote about the dangers of smoking tobacco. He called it 'loathsome to the eye, hateful to the nose, harmful to the brain and dangerous to the lungs'. He wrote with some sense, didn't he?

Beliefs about being king: He believed that God had chosen him to be king – an idea called the '**Divine Right of Kings**'. He thought that even God Himself called kings 'gods' and said that no one could argue with him because that would be like arguing with God – something that nobody would ever dream of doing.

Fashion: He wore padded clothes in case anyone tried to stab him. And if he got holes in an outfit he wouldn't change it, he'd just pull another item of clothing over the top!

Hygiene: He never washed. A man who knew the King, Sir Anthony Weldon, once wrote that 'his tongue was too large for his mouth and his drink came out of each side of his mouth and dribbled back into the cup'.

Manners: He swore all the time, picked his nose and used his sleeve as a handkerchief when he had a cold.

Nicknames: None at the time but in 1625, Sir Anthony Weldon said, 'he was crafty and cunning in small things but a fool in important matters'. I bet Sir Anthony could have thought up a few nicknames. Someone also described the King as a 'nervous drivelling idiot' a few years later.

'Kings and Queens are the most supreme things on earth. Kings are God's lieutenants. They exercise a manner of divine power on earth. To dispute that God may do is **blasphemy** – so it is **sedition** for ordinary citizens to dispute what a king might do.'

↵ **SOURCE A:**
James I, from a speech to Parliament in 1610.

'... he was a clever man but did not have Elizabeth's skills in dealing with people. They blamed him for giving favourites too much power, spending too much money at court and quarrelling with Parliament. They said he was unpleasant and cowardly.'

↵ **SOURCE B:**
From 'The making of the UK' by James Mason, 1992.

The first union flag – 1606.

These designs were rejected.

↵ **SOURCE C:**
James quickly labelled himself King of Great Britain, although England and Scotland still ran on their own affairs. In 1606, a competition was held to find a new flag that united both countries – the union flag.

WISE-UP Words

blasphemy
Divine Right of Kings
sedition

When James I (VI of Scotland) arrived in England in 1603 he knew that one of his most important problems would be one that had troubled England's kings and queens for years – religion. As usual, people still quarrelled about religion (as they always had done) but clever Queen Elizabeth had worked hard to stop arguments between Catholics and Protestants.

But when James met up with church leaders in 1604, he failed to impress them. Some strict Protestants were so unhappy with the meeting that they left England forever. He also angered the Catholics when he ordered all their 'troublesome' priests to leave England. One small group of Catholics was so angry that they decided to launch one of the most famous murder plans in history – the Gunpowder Plot.

The new king also managed to fall out with Parliament in a big way. James needed Parliament to help him rule – but didn't want them to argue with him about anything. When Parliament refused to collect money for the king, James sent all the politicians home… for 10 years!

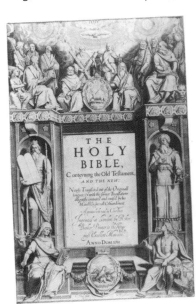

Instead, James asked his friend for help running the country – and found other ways to get money, like selling land and titles! However, despite managing to find ways to get lots of cash, James was even better at spending it – and by the time of his death in 1625, the King was nearly bankrupt.

↵ **SOURCE D:** *When James met with church leaders at Hampton Court Palace in 1604, it was agreed that a new English translation of the Bible, as it became known, remained unchanged for 300 years and has been the most printed book in history!*

Work

1 On Queen Elizabeth's death, why was the King of Scotland asked to become King of England?

2 a Look at the fact file on James I, paying particular attention to the portrait. Write a description of James I's appearance.

   b Give a reason why this painting might not show the truth about James.

   c How does Sir Anthony Weldon describe James?

   d Sir Anthony had worked for James but was sacked by him in 1617. Does this make any difference to how we should treat his opinions?

3 Look at Source B.

   a In your own words, explain what is meant by the 'Divine Right of Kings'.

   b Why do you think James was so keen on the 'Divine Right of Kings'?

   c Why do you think Members of Parliament would not be as keen on it?

4 Design your own flag to represent the union of England and Scotland under one king. Remember though – both the English and the Scots would have to like it.

5 Imagine you were a foreign visitor who had just visited England (and met King James) in 1605. Write a short report about him to send home.

——MISSION ACCOMPLISHED?——

- Can you explain what the 'Divine Right of Kings' was?
- Do you know five facts about King James I of England?

Remember, remember the fifth of November!

_____ MISSION OBJECTIVES _____

- To know at least five accepted facts about the Gunpowder Plot and also to understand why it is difficult to get a clear picture of the Plot.

Remember, remember, the fifth of November
Gunpowder, treason and plot.
I see no reason why gunpowder, treason,
Should ever be forgot...

Most of you will have heard this poem – at least the first two lines anyway. It commemorates an event so famous that millions of people all over the country still remember it – over 400 years after it happened. That legendary event is the Gunpowder Plot.

The Gunpowder Plot of 1605 has all the ingredients of a brilliant crime story. A plan to kill the King, gunpowder, betrayal, prison, torture, gun battles, hangings and fireworks. What a story!

Most of you will know the story quite well. Your friends and family will probably know the same tale. But do you know the full story? Was Guy Fawkes 'set up'? Did King James know about the assassination plot all along?

These two pages outline the familiar story of the Gunpowder Plot, the one you probably know already. The pages that follow (pages 82 and 83) then look at the evidence in detail. Then you will be challenged to make up your own mind – were the gunpowder plotters framed?

King James I

In 1605, there were laws passed against people who were Catholic. King James had even ordered Catholic priests to leave England or face execution. A small group of Catholics decided that they wanted James dead. They hoped a new king or queen would treat them better.

PLAN A:
Early in 1604, Thomas Percy rented a house next to Parliament. The gang tried to tunnel under Parliament, just below where the King would sit. However, the tunnel soon filled with water.

↰ SOURCE A: *A picture of the plotters. It is unlikely that the artist ever saw the men.*

PLAN B:
In spring 1605, Percy rented a cellar directly under Parliament. Thirty-six barrels of gunpowder were smuggled in and stored behind the piles of wood.

The Plot

Every year, the king or queen officially opened Parliament. In 1605, Parliament was due to be opened on 5 November and most of the powerful people in the country would go to watch – this ceremony still takes place today. The plot was to blow up the King when he was in Parliament, seize his young daughter, Elizabeth, who lived in the Midlands and place her on the throne instead of James. Obviously, she would need help from older people, who would be Catholic of course.

The plotters

Their leader was the brave and handsome Robert Catesby. He was a devout Catholic who had gambled away much of his family's wealth. He was joined by Tom and Robert Winter, the Wright brothers (Chris and John), Thomas Percy and of course Guido – or Guy – Fawkes. Guy was an experienced soldier who was used to handling explosives. He would be responsible for lighting the gunpowder to be placed under Parliament. There were also many others who knew of the plan too.

What went wrong?

On 26 October 1605, a mysterious letter arrived at the house of a man called Lord Monteagle. The note contained a warning:

'I warn you… To devise some excuse to shift your attendance at the Parliament… they shall receive a terrible blow this Parliament and yet they shall not see who hurts them…'

Monteagle immediately took the note to Robert Cecil, who was the King's chief advisor. Cecil took the letter to the King.

Just after midnight on 5 November, the cellars below Parliament were searched. A tall, brown-haired man was found hanging around. He was holding a lantern and had with him a watch, matches and a tinderbox in his pockets. He said his name was John Johnson and that he worked for Thomas Percy. He was brought before King James but refused to answer any of his questions. The King then ordered that he be taken to the Tower of London and questioned. After two days of torture on the rack he gave his real name as Guido Fawkes. After another two days he told his torturers that he was there to blow up Parliament. After another six days, he named the other plotters.

⬑ SOURCE B: *A terrible punishment for the plotters.*

What about the others?

When the other plotters realised the plan hadn't worked, they barricaded themselves in Holbeach House, near Dudley in the Midlands. They tried to dry out some of their wet gunpowder near a fire and, not surprisingly, it blew up. The noise from the explosion alerted the King's troops, who were searching nearby. After a shoot-out in which both Catesby and Percy were killed by the same bullet, the surviving plotters were arrested and taken to London. However, some would say Catesby and Percy were the lucky ones…

The punishment

After a quick trial, the survivors, including Guy Fawkes, were sentenced to death. They were dragged through the streets of London, hanged until they were nearly dead, cut down, cut open and their insides were pulled out and burned on a fire in front of them. Then their corpses were cut ⎯ pieces and put on display around the country.

! FACT Clever Guy!
Guy Fawkes was probably dead before his punishment properly began. As he climbed up the scaffold steps with the hangman's noose around his neck, he jumped off, head first and broke his neck. The execution carried on regardless.

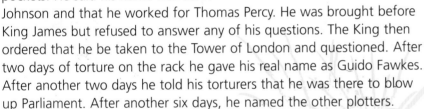
Work

1 Explain what the plotters hoped to achieve by blowing up King James.

2 Write down the names of all the people involved in the Gunpowder Plot. Next to each one, write down the role they played, for example, Lord Monteagle – was sent the letter warning him of the plot to blow up Parliament.

3 a Read the passage taken from the unsigned letter to Lord Monteagle.

   b In your own words, explain the meaning of the letter.

4 Why do you think King James ordered such a nasty execution for the plotters?

5 Imagine you were in London to witness the execution of Guy Fawkes and the remaining Catholic plotters. Write a letter to a friend describing the events of that day. Remember, at the time most people were pleased that the plot had failed.

6 How do many people remember the Gunpowder Plot today?

Were the Gunpowder plotters framed?

MISSION OBJECTIVES

- To act as a 'history-mystery detective' and come to a conclusion as to whether you think the Gunpowder plotters were set up.

For hundreds of years, people believed the official government story of the Gunpowder Plot. Most people still believe this story today. It is the story that you have read on pages 80 and 81. However, in recent years, some historians have found it difficult to accept this story. It has been argued that Robert Cecil, the King's minister and advisor, found out about the plot and even encouraged it. Cecil was a Protestant who wanted to make Catholics as unpopular as possible – what better way to do this than uncover a Catholic plot to kill the King?

Look carefully through the following evidence. Your task is to hunt for clues, piece them together and try to establish a clear picture of the plot to kill King James.

EVIDENCE A
The 36 barrels of gunpowder were kept in a cellar next to Parliament. The cellar was rented to Thomas Percy by John Whynniard, a friend of Robert Cecil. Whynniard died suddenly and unexpectedly on the morning of 5 November.

EVIDENCE B
All supplies of gunpowder were kept under guard in the Tower of London. The records for 1604 are missing.

EVIDENCE C
Lord Monteagle took the warning letter to Robert Cecil on 27 October. The cellars below Parliament weren't searched until at least a week later.

EVIDENCE D
According to a Catholic visitor to London in 1604, Robert Cecil said:

'The King is too kind to Catholics. This gives great offence to others. We cannot hope for good government while we have a large number of people who obey foreign rulers as Catholics do. The Catholic priests preach that Catholics must even kill the King to help their religion.'

EVIDENCE E
Two examples of Guy Fawkes' signature whilst he was in the Tower of London. One was written just after his arrest; the other was scribbled a few days later. Why do you think the signatures are so different?

EVIDENCE F

Part of Thomas Winter's confession, read out at the trial. The original confession has never been seen. A copy was written out by Robert Cecil for the trial.

'We were working under a little entry to the Parliament house. We under-propped it with wood. We bought the gunpowder and hid it in Mr Percy's house. We worked another two weeks against the stone wall, which was very hard to get through. At that time we called in Kit Wright. About Easter we rented the cellar. After this Mr Fawkes laid into the cellar 1000 sticks and 500 faggots.'

Note: A faggot is an old word for a bundle of firewood.

EVIDENCE G

The cellars below Parliament were searched on 4 November. Guards discovered a man next to piles of wood. He told them he was John Johnson. He wasn't arrested.

EVIDENCE H

One of the plotters, Francis Tresham, was Monteagle's brother-in-law. He was the only plotter who was not captured quickly. He was only caught on 12 December. He died of a mysterious illness on 22 December, locked away in the Tower of London. Some said he'd been poisoned.

EVIDENCE I

Holbeach House was surrounded on 7 November, only two days after Fawkes was captured. According to the government report, it took them two days of torture to get Fawkes to reveal his real name, let alone his part in the plot (another two days) and the names of the plotters (a further six days).

Work

Now you have read all the evidence, it is time to put together your theory about the Gunpowder Plot.

STEP 1 Find evidence that the plotters were framed

Can you find any evidence of a connection between the plot and Robert Cecil? Has Cecil tried to hide anything? Perhaps even tried to stop people from talking? Did he know details of the plot before it happened? Make notes on what you have discovered.

STEP 2 Find a motive

The King was not very popular with his subjects at the time. Can you find any evidence to suggest why Cecil would set up Catholic plotters and only catch them at the last minute? Write down your findings.

STEP 3 Think! Can we trust the evidence?

Is there any reason not to trust the confessions of the plotters who were caught – are they reliable? If not, why not? Write down the ideas that you have.

STEP 4 Time to wake up your mind, history detective! Were the plotters framed?

Write a short paragraph outlining your theory – was Cecil involved in setting up the plotters? Be sure to back up your ideas with some of the evidence.

MISSION ACCOMPLISHED?

- Can you list at least five accepted facts about the Gunpowder Plot?
- Can you explain why it is difficult for historians to get a clear picture of events in history?

Which witch is which?

- To understand what sort of people were accused of witchcraft in Stuart England... and why they were accused.

People in Tudor and Stuart England were a very superstitious bunch. The day Queen Elizabeth was crowned, for example, was only specially selected after the stars had been studied for several weeks! Despite the fact that scientists were uncovering more and more about the world, people still didn't understand how animals could suddenly drop down dead or why a field of crops might fail one year. More often than not, when bad things happened in a town or village, it was concluded that a witch was at work. Witches, people thought, were the Devil's own helpers, always on the lookout to do evil things and help sinners to find their way to hell!

King James I himself was very interested in witchcraft and even wrote a book, suggesting different ways to catch witches. He famously wrote that all witches had strange marks on their bodies where they fed their 'familiars'. A 'familiar' was a small creature – a toad or a cat – that sucked on the witch's blood every night. The 'familiar', James wrote, was really the Devil himself in disguise! In fact, all sorts of 'witch-spotting' tips were published – they had no shadow, they talked to themselves, their hair couldn't be cut, they couldn't say the Lord's Prayer without making a mistake and many more.

King James told Parliament to pass strict laws against anybody who was thought to be a witch and, in 1604, witchcraft became a crime punishable by hanging! Over the next 100 years, thousands of people were accused of witchcraft. Most were poor and, not surprisingly, the majority were old women – after all, they were the most likely to live alone with a pet and have strange marks on their body from a lifetime of hard work!

In James I's book, he claimed that a sure-fire way to identify a witch was to 'swim' them. The swimming test, pictured above in a print from 1612, was a kind of trial. The accused would have their arms tied in front of them and a rope strapped around their waist. They would then be thrown into a pond that would have been 'blessed' by a priest. The test determined that if the accused floated, they must be a witch because the 'pure' water didn't want them. They would be hanged. If they sank, the 'pure' water wanted them so they must be pure themselves and couldn't possibly be a witch – they were declared innocent (but dead!).

↳ SOURCE A: *'Swimming' a suspected witch.*

Witch-hunting was at its height in East Anglia during 14 terrible months between 1645 and 1646. An unsuccessful lawyer named Matthew Hopkins set up his own witch-hunt, claiming that he had the Devil's own personal list of witches in England. Over two years, hundreds of people were rounded up as a result of his enquiries – and most were old women over the age of 50! He had 68 people put to death in Bury St Edmunds alone and 19 hanged in Chelmsford, Essex, in a single day. In fact, during these years, there were more cases of witchcraft in Essex courts than of any other crime, apart from theft. After Essex, Hopkins set off for Norfolk and Suffolk. The town of Aldeburgh paid him £6 for clearing the town of witches. In King's Lynn, he got £15 and in Stowmarket he received £23. And this was at a time when the average daily wage was two pence!

During the seventeenth century, about 2000 people were hanged as witches in England, Wales and Scotland before the 'witch craze' finally began to die down. Witchcraft ceased to be a crime in 1736. England's last victim, Alice Molland, was executed for witchcraft in 1727. Apparently, she had turned her missing daughter into a flying horse!

↳ **SOURCE B:** *A print from a book of the time featuring Matthew Hopkins. He called himself the 'Witch Finder General' and he is pictured here surrounded by several 'familiars'.*

SOURCE D: *Genuine examples of people accused of witchcraft. Each of these people was hanged for their 'crimes'.* ↱

SOURCE C: *A German painting, dated 1555, showing witches burning on a bonfire. The craze for hunting witches never got as bad in England as it did in other countries. Some historians think that around 200 000 people were tortured, burned or hanged for witchcraft in Europe between 1500 and 1750!* ↘

Work ~~~~~~.

1 Look at Source A.

   a In your own words, explain how the 'swimming test' was meant to identify a witch. Include details about the reasons and logic behind the test.

   b Do you think this was a fair test? Write down the reasons for your answer.

2 a Write down five facts about the 'Witch Finder General'.

   b Imagine the Witch Finder General himself is coming to your town and you want to impress him. Design a booklet that gives details about your town's efforts to catch witches. Include:
   • information about spotting a witch;
   • successful convictions;
   • drawings to show your witch trials.

3 Look at Source D.

   a For each of the people in the source, write down the reasons why you think they were accused of being a witch.

   b How would you explain each of the events in the source today?

Alice Mullholland: a poor woman who gathered sticks on someone else's land. When told to stop, she threw the sticks down in temper and mumbled something under her breath. Nothing ever grew in that spot again. She was often seen moving her lips in church and could sometimes predict whether it would rain or shine.

Mother Samuel: an old lady who put a spell on two children who were having fits, Samuel claimed they were just naughty boys. The local landowner's wife once tried to cut her hair but Mother Samuel pulled away. The wife began to feel sick.

Thomas Papley: a poor man who owned two vicious cats. He also fed birds. One day, the man's cat frightened a pig. The pig then danced in an odd way and died.

MISSION ACCOMPLISHED?

• Can you explain what are meant by the terms 'witch', 'familiar' and 'witches mark'?

Why do Americans speak English?

• To discover why and how the English began to settle in North America.

Ever wondered why English is the most common language used in North America? After all, America is thousands of miles away from England, over the Atlantic ocean – so why do most Americans speak English?

The story of the English language in America starts in Tudor and Stuart times. Read the following cartoons carefully.

For thousands of years Native American (or Red Indian) tribes lived in North America.

Great civilizations like the Aztecs and Incas could be found in Central and South America too.

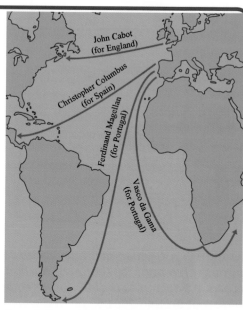

In 1492 Christopher Columbus became the first recorded European to 'discover' the Americas. He was an Italian who was sponsored by Spain.

Other famous sailors followed Columbus but it was Spain and Portugal who began to dominate the world of exploration.

By the mid 1500s. Spain controlled lots of land in the Americas including Cuba, Panama, Jamaica, Chile, Ecuador, Peru and North-West Argentina.

Whilst Spain could boast of finding gold, tobacco, potatoes, tomatoes, cotton, sugar and rum in their new colonies. England had to be content with sailing to the Northern part of North America... and finding cod.

With Spain controlling most of the trading routes to central and South America. England's monarchs encouraged their sailors to concentrate on North America and trying to find a route to the Spice Islands and India above Russia and what we now call Canada.

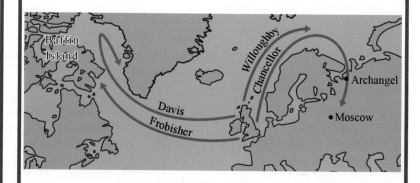

Famous Englishmen like Hugh Willoughby, Richard Chancellor Martin Frobisher and John Davis each got reputations as fantastic explorers and sailors.

In 1584, Queen Elizabeth gave permission to one of her favourites, Walter Raleigh, to start a settlement – or colony – in North America.

It was called Virginia after a name Elizabeth was known by – the Virgin Queen.

Over 100 settlers (or colonists) from England tried to start new lives in this new English **colony** but there was no good harbour, no easy way to make money and the local native tribesman were hostile!

When, after a few years, Raleigh tried to start another colony in North America, all new settlers found were the skeletons of the people from the first voyages.

! FACT Names, names, names

European settlers in North America called the local tribesmen 'Indians' or 'Redskins'. Some tribes were aggressive; others were peaceful, like Squanto and his people. As more European settlers arrived, some tried to wipe out the tribes. Today, we don't call them 'Indians' or 'Redskins'. They are known as **Native Americans**.

In April 1607 a group of English settlers tried to settle in America again by moving to Virginia.

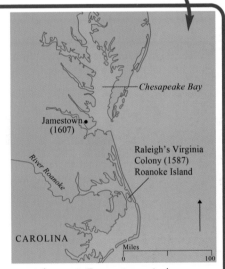

They named their new settlement Jamestown in honour of King James I but they struggled to survive. By September 1607, half of the 104 colonists had died from disease and the local tribespeople remained hostile.

In September 1620, 102 men women and children tried yet again to start a new life in North America.

Thirty-five of the travellers were Puritans, unhappy with King James I, who would not adopt their ideas about how God should be worshiped. A person who undertakes a religious journey is known as a pilgrim. The Puritans were sometimes called pilgrims. Americans today are very proud of these hardworking settlers of 1620, who helped found their nation. They are known in American history books as the 'Pilgrim Fathers' or the 'Founding Fathers'.

! FACT Who were the Puritans?

Puritans were members of the Church of England (Protestants) but they still believed that more change in religion was needed. They felt that the Protestant Church still allowed too much sin to take place, like playing football on a Sunday when people should be praying. Puritans tried to lead 'pure' lives. They followed the word of the Bible and wanted plain and simple services to take place in simple churches.

Their voyage in a small ship called the *Mayflower* lasted over two months. Food supplies went rotten and storms threw them off course.

Finally they saw land on 11 December and started to build a small town where they came ashore. They named it Plymouth because they had set sail from Plymouth in England.

Life in their new home was hard. They struggled to grow food – crops of English wheat and peas failed. Fifty-one settlers died in the first winter from diseases such as pneumonia.

But the settlers were determined to survive and in the spring of 1621 they received help from an unexpected source.

A local native tribesman called Squanto showed the settlers how to plant 20 acres of corn and six acres of barley correctly.

He advised them how to fertilise the soil with dead fish! From then on the settlers knew how to farm properly and life started to improve.

By 1624, over 120 people, including more settlers from England, were living in Plymouth, New England.

To celebrate their successful harvest – and to give thanks to God for their good fortune – the settlers tucked into a feast of turkey and goose. They invited the local tribesmen to join them.

This first meal enjoyed together by tribesmen and the settlers is still remembered in North America today.

Every November, millions of American families have a day off work and sit down to a family meal of turkey or goose, cranberry sauce and pumpkin pie.

The success of the 1620 settlers encouraged others to leave England and move to the 'new world'.

They were joined by Dutch, French, and settlers from other countries. In fact, Dutch settlers were responsible for building a town called New Amsterdam… later renamed New York!

Despite the settlers from many other nations, it was the English who began to dominate the area – and take over more and more land.

Soon, products grown in America, such as tobacco, cotton and sugar began to flood into England, Wales and Scotland – making people on both sides of the Atlantic Ocean very rich.

By 1700 there were 13 English colonies in North America – remembered today by 13 stripes on the US flag.

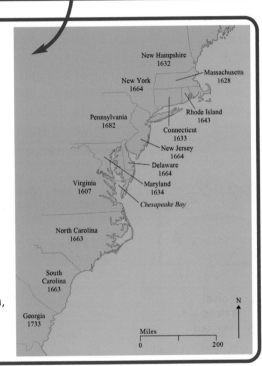

It was now clear that English men, women and children – and the English language – were firmly rooted in North America.

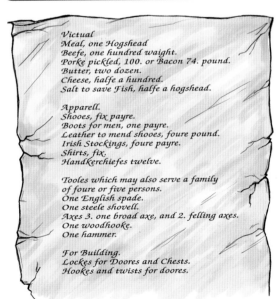

↵ **SOURCE A:** *A list of things that a settler family was advised to take to America.*

WISE-UP Words

colony
Native Americans
Pilgrim Fathers

Work

1 a Write a sentence or two about each of the following:
  • the Puritans;
  • their reasons for leaving England;
  • their journey on the *Mayflower*;
  • the problems with their new home.

b Who helped the settlers with one of their problems?

c How did he help?

2 Look at Source A.

a List five foods, five items of clothing and five tools that settlers had to take with them.

b Why did some settlers not have to take as much as others?

c Why do you think the settlers had to bring so much equipment and food?

3 Imagine you are a settler who has briefly returned to England in 1620. People are constantly asking you what it is like in the New World. Prepare a speech to give to a group of Puritans unsure whether to take the trip. Try to convince them that travelling with you on your return journey is a good idea.

4 a How does 'Thanksgiving Day' get its name?

b How did the 'Pilgrim Fathers' get their name?

MISSION ACCOMPLISHED?

• Can you explain the terms 'Pilgrim Fathers', 'Thanksgiving Day' and 'colony'?

ENGLAND AT WAR

In 1642, thousands of Englishmen went to war. They weren't going to fight the French, the Spanish or any other foreign country. They went to fight OTHER Englishmen. England was at war with itself. We call this a civil war. So what made English turn against each other? What were the two sides called? And how was the country divided?

1: Why did the English Civil War start?

MISSION OBJECTIVES

- To know why King Charles I, son of James I, had become so unpopular.
- To understand who the Royalists and the Parliamentarians were.
- To know what a civil war is.

In most wars, there are two sides facing each other. The English Civil War was no different. On one side were King Charles I and his followers, known as the **Royalists**. They fought the men of Parliament and their followers. This group was known as the **Parliamentarians**. For many years, as you will know, Parliament had worked with the king or queen.

They helped make laws, discussed wars and raised taxes. However, firstly James I and then his son Charles I, had begun to argue regularly with Parliament. They thought that Parliament was there to serve them… but Parliament thought differently. They thought that the monarch was there to serve his or her country! The argument would end in war.

King Charles I

I am the King and I can do as I like. This is my **divine right** because God has appointed me. Parliament thinks it can control its king by keeping me short of money. Parliament must be stopped… even if it means war.

Running England is a difficult job and Parliament has been helping kings and queens for years. We like helping to make decisions but Charles only uses us to collect taxes for him. When we last refused to get him any more money, he sent us all home for 11 years and ruled without us. He only asked us back because a Scottish army invaded and Charles needed money to raise an army. It was even Charles' fault because he told them to use a new prayer book they didn't like. Charles must change his ways… even if it means war.

A Member of Parliament

A rich lord

If Charles needs money, Parliament must get it for him. He is their king and God has put him on the throne. Parliament must allow a king to act like a king but they don't give him enough money. Parliament even ordered the execution of two of Charles' personal advisors. Parliament must be stopped… even if it means war.

A Puritan

There are more of us than ever before. Our 'pure' way of worship is becoming popular and many of us are Members of Parliament now. Charles even married a young Catholic princess – is he trying to make the country more Catholic? We must stop him... even if it means war.

A farm worker

I will have to fight for Charles because my landlord told me to. He told me that Charles was appointed by God and I don't want to go against God's wishes. If Parliament is against Charles, they must be against God. They must be stopped... even if it means war.

A merchant

I work very hard to make a good living. But Charles takes taxes from us without asking. His most recent idea was a charge for living by or near the sea. He calls it a **ship tax**. Charles must be stopped... even if it means war.

WISE-UP Words

civil war
divine right
Parliamentarian
Royalist   ship tax

The final straw came when Parliament sent Charles a long list of complaints about him and his way of running the country. He was furious. He took 300 soldiers to London to arrest the five most troublesome Members of Parliament. However, when he got there, they had all escaped. Charles then left London and headed north to collect his army together. His queen went to Holland to sell the crown jewels to pay for the war. Parliament started to bring its own army together. The English Civil War was about to begin.

Work

1 a Explain what is meant by the following words:

  Royalist • Parliamentarian • divine right

  b What is the main difference between an ordinary war and a 'civil' war?

2 Copy the following statements into your book. Beside each, you must write either the word ROYALIST (if it would be the view of the supporter of the King) or write PARLIAMENT (if this view would be held by a supporter of rule by Parliament):

  • The King is chosen by God – he has a divine right to rule.
  • Parliament's job is to follow the King's commands.
  • No King of England should marry a foreign Catholic.
  • The King is there to serve his country – not the other way around!
  • One man cannot govern an entire nation.
  • This ship tax is unfair and illegal.

  Are any statements believable by both sides?

3 Could the Civil War have been avoided? What decisions could either side have made that could have stopped a war before it started?

4 Which side is most to blame for the Civil War – the King or Parliament? Give reasons for your answer.

——— MISSION ACCOMPLISHED? ———

• Do you know two reasons why Charles I became unpopular with some of his people?
• Do you know which side the Royalists supported?

On 22 August 1642, King Charles gathered his army and stuck his Royal Standard (a big flag!) into the ground in a field near Nottingham. It was the signal that the English Civil War had started. So what kind of people made up Charles' army? Who dared to fight against their king? And how did the two armies fight and work out who was on each side?

2: Match of the day: Roundheads versus Cavaliers

MISSION OBJECTIVES

- To understand which sections of society supported each side in the Civil War.
- To know how soldiers fought in the Civil War and what they looked like.

Not too many people actually chose which side they were going to be on. They supported the side that got to their town or village first, or the side their local lord supported. Friends would end up fighting friends; fathers might fight against their sons and so on. A woman might be married to a Parliamentarian but be sister to a Royalist! Civil wars were very nasty affairs. However, some groups of people knew exactly who they would fight for!

Royalists (Cavaliers)

Parliamentarians (Roundheads)

The rich lords and country gentlemen usually fought for the King. His support was strongest in the North of England, Wales, Devon, Cornwall and Somerset. Parliament was most popular in the south, especially London and other large towns and ports. Merchants, businessmen and any Puritans would fight for Parliament.

The richer gentlemen on each side went into battle on horseback. The **cavalry**, as soldiers on horseback are known, wore steel breastplates over their leather coats. They tried to break through the enemy lines by firing their pistols and cutting men down with their swords.

Ordinary people on each side joined either the pikemen or the musketeers. Soldiers without horses were also known as **infantry** or footsoldiers. As you couldn't tell who your enemy was by their appearance or language, both sides wore brightly coloured strips of cloth. The Royalists wore red **sashes** and the Parliamentarians wore yellow ones. That way, you could clearly see who was on each side – just like on a football pitch!

❚❚ PAUSE for Thought

Why do you think businessmen and any people living in or around a port would decide to fight against the King?

The pikemen

These boys were tough! The **pikeman**'s job was to stand at the front of the whole army with a 5m-long pole, a **pike**, tipped with steel. As the enemy approached, they dug one end into the ground and pointed the other at the charging enemy's horse. They wore heavy armour (who could blame them!) and also carried a sword.

The musketeers

A **musket** was a big clumsy gun. It was so heavy that **musketeers** (the men who fired them) needed a stick to rest it on! The gun was fired by using a 'match' (a piece of burning rope) to light the gunpowder that had been poured into the barrel. Hopefully, a ball or shot would fly out and travel up to 400m. It was all a slow, complicated and very dangerous job – there was always a chance of accidentally blowing a finger off. One Royalist musketeer said, 'We seem to bury more fingers and thumbs than we do men.'

There were 635 different clashes between **Cavaliers** and **Roundheads** during the English Civil War. Sometimes the Cavaliers won, sometimes there was no clear winner and, on other occasions, the Roundheads claimed victory. One Royalist general and his troops even changed sides – but forgot to change the red sashes to the new Roundhead yellow ones. They were all shot by their new **allies**.

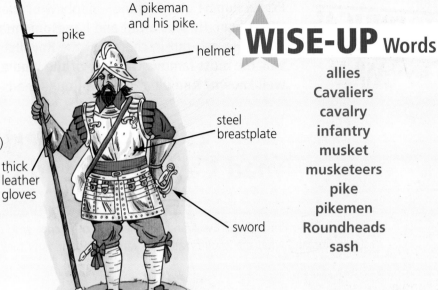

A pikeman and his pike.

pike · helmet · steel breastplate · thick leather gloves · sword

A musketeer and his musket. He would use his weapon as a club when the enemy got close.

musket · match · bullet pouch · rest · gunpowder cases

WISE-UP Words

allies
Cavaliers
cavalry
infantry
musket
musketeers
pike
pikemen
Roundheads
sash

✚ Hungry for MORE

For either a musketeer or a pikeman, write a job description in order to try and recruit more members of your army. Try to include the following:
• details of the job and responsibilities;
• equipment supplied;
• hazards of the job;
• benefits of the job.

Work

1 Explain each of the following words:
   Roundheads • Cavaliers • cavalry • infantry
   • musketeer • pikeman • allies

2 Look at the pictures of the pikeman and the musketeer. On which side did each fight? Explain how you made your choice.

3 a Draw and label a picture of one of the soldiers.
   b Explain how your soldier would fight.

MISSION ACCOMPLISHED?

• Could you explain to people what kind of person fought for the Cavaliers?
• Do you know who fought in the Roundhead armies?
• Can you name two weapons used on the Civil War battlefield and the names of the soldiers who used them?

Prince Rupert of the Rhine – nephew of the King – was 23 years old when the Civil War began. He was a tall and handsome man who had been a soldier from the age of 13! He was put in charge of the Royalist Cavalry and, apart from Charles himself, was the most famous Cavalier of the whole war. So what did he do to become so well known? And what did the Roundheads think of him?

3: Prince Rupert – mad Cavalier or sad Cavalier?

MISSION OBJECTIVES

- To know who Prince Rupert was and why he was so popular with the King's supporters.
- To understand what the Roundheads thought of him and how they tried to damage his reputation.

Rupert won fans because:

- He was brave and fearless. He led brilliant cavalry charges and managed to capture several towns that supported Parliament.
  October 1642: Led the King's cavalry during battle of Edgehill. Battle was drawn.
  March 1643: Stopped Roundheads taking over Royalist Oxford.
  July 1643: Captured Bristol.
  May 1644: Captured other major ports.
  June 1644: Saved York from Roundhead attack.

- His best friend was his little white poodle called 'Boy'. The dog went everywhere with Rupert, even into battle.

Rupert was greatly admired by the Royalists and they lovingly nicknamed him the 'Mad Cavalier'. However, as you might expect, the Roundheads hated him.

During battles, Roundheads looked carefully across the battlefield to spot him. It would have lifted their spirits to have killed Rupert… but no one seemed to be able to get near him. The Roundheads were also very **superstitious** about his dog, saying it was an evil spirit whose mother was a witch. Roundhead soldiers claimed that they had heard the dog talking (in several different languages) and that he had the power to make himself invisible. They thought that Boy's powers made his master unbeatable!

By the end of the year 1644, Rupert had avoided all attempts to kill him. Boy wasn't so lucky. He wandered onto the battlefield at Marston Moor in 1644 and was shot. Although the Roundheads never wounded Rupert in battle, they tried to wound him with words and pictures. This is known as **propaganda** and throughout history people have used it to say what they feel about other people. Things are written or drawn to give a message about someone. The writer or artist often makes things up too!

Look at the following sources very carefully. Each is about Prince Rupert and/or his dog. Think about the propaganda message that the writer or artist was trying to put across.

WISE-UP Words

plundering
propaganda superstitious

SOURCE A:
A portrait of Prince Rupert. ↱

SOURCE B: *A description of what Prince Rupert and his troops did in Birmingham, April 1643. It was written by the wife of a Parliamentary commander.*

'They ran into every house cursing and damning, threatening and terrifying the poor women most terribly, setting naked swords and pistols to their breasts. They fell to **plundering** all the town, picking purses and pockets, searching in holes and corners and every other place they could suspect for money or goods. They beastly assaulted many women... and bragged about it afterwards, how many they had ravished. The next day in every street they kindled fire with gunpowder, matches, wisps of straw and burning coals.'

SOURCE C: *'Prince Rupert and the Royalists capture a town'. Drawn by a man who supported Parliament.*

SOURCE D: *This drawing by a Parliamentarian shows Rupert hiding in a field after defeat at Marston Moor in 1644. Look for: i) Roundheads capturing his baggage and wagons and discovering objects used by Catholics; ii) His dead pet poodle, Boy. He has been painted black to show he was dead.*

'Sad Cavaliers,
Rupert invites all you survivors
To his dog's funeral
Close mourners are the witch, Pope and devil,
Who regret the death of the late fallen evil.'

SOURCE E: *A poem taken from a leaflet printed to celebrate Boy's death.*

Work

1 a Why do you think Roundhead soldiers hated Prince Rupert so much?

b Were the Roundheads successful in killing Prince Rupert?

2 a Explain what is meant by the word 'propaganda'.

b Read Source B. Why might this source be an example of propaganda?

c What is the propaganda message in Source C?

d Can historians be sure that the events in Sources B and C actually took place? Give reasons for your answer.

3 Read Source E.
Do you think this poem was written by a Royalist or a Parliamentarian? Give reasons for your answer.

4 Throughout the Civil War, the Roundheads tried hard to capture Prince Rupert. At one point they offered a reward for his capture… and his dog! Design a 'Wanted' poster for Prince Rupert and Boy. Try to include some examples of Roundhead propaganda in your design.

MISSION ACCOMPLISHED?

- Could you tell someone why some people admired Prince Rupert?
- Do you know one reason why some Roundheads were scared of him?
- Can you explain how the Parliamentarians used propaganda to change what people thought about Rupert?

The first great battle of the Civil War – Edgehill in 1642 – ended in a draw. The commanders of Parliament's armies were shocked by the lack of discipline and skill shown by their troops. This was the first fighting that many of the soldiers had seen and they had been given very little training. In the chaos of battle, orders were ignored, soldiers fled in panic and it was impossible to control what the army was doing. The King's cavalry were experienced and well trained and very nearly wiped Parliament's forces out. So how did the Roundhead commanders react? What changes did they make to their forces? And what was it like to live and fight in the New Model Army?

4: What was new about the New Model Army?

MISSION OBJECTIVES

- To understand why Parliament needed to improve its army.
- To know who was responsible for the training of Parliament's New Model Army.
- To be able to understand how their strict discipline made them a more effective fighting force.

Parliament turned to a Puritan Member of Parliament and farmer from Norfolk called Oliver Cromwell. They gave him the job of training a new set of troops to take on the King's men. This new fighting force was England's first truly professional army and, as it was a different kind of army, was given the name, the New Model Army. Cromwell made his troops live according to the rules of his religion and harshly punished anyone who broke his laws. Read through the following sources carefully.

'These men were strictly trained and strictly disciplined. But above all, they fought for God. Singing hymns, they charged into battle and their discipline proved too much for Rupert's cavalry, for although the cavaliers were good horsemen, they were not always good soldiers.'

↳ **SOURCE A:** *A view of the New Model Army from a history textbook, 'History Alive Book 1', by Peter Moss (1980).*

'Give me a russet-coated captain who knows what he fights for and loves what he knows, than that which you call a gentlemen and is nothing else.'

↳ **SOURCE B:** *Cromwell said this in 1644. It shows that he chose his men based on their abilities rather than their wealth. 'Russet' was the reddish-brown colour of the New Model Army's coats.*

'Cromwell taught his cavalrymen to care for their horses and clean their weapons... regular drill [training] and strict discipline made his cavalry more manoeuvrable [easier to control] than the Royalist cavalry.'

↳ **SOURCE C:** *From 'Oliver Cromwell and His World', by Maurice Ashley (1972).*

The secret of success

All that training and discipline paid off at the Battles of Marston Moor (1644) and Naseby (1645). Both were crushing victories for Parliament and at Naseby, the King's army was all but destroyed by a series of complicated moves and brave attacks by Cromwell's men. On 5 May 1645, King Charles I realised he had no answer to these russet-coated troops. He surrendered to Scotland, hoping he would be safe north of the border. But the Scottish sold him to Parliament for a massive £400 000! The King was taken as a prisoner of Parliament to the Isle of Wight. They had beaten his armies and had taken him prisoner – what were they going to do with him next?

Lawes of the Army

Duties to God –
First let no man Blaspheme [swear] our Christian Faith, upon paine to have his tongue bored with a red-hot iron.

Duties towards Superiors and Commanders –
Resisting against correction – No man shall resist, draw, lift or offer to draw, or lift his weapon against any officer.
Seditiuos [criticising Cromwell or Parliament] **words –**
None shall utter any words of sedition and uproar, or mutiny, upon pain of death.

Moral duties –
Unnatural abuses – Rapes, ravishments, unnatural abuses, shall be punished with death.
Theft – Theft and robbery, exceeding the value of twelve pence, shall be punished with death.

Duties towards civilians [ordinary people not involved in the fighting] –
Waste and extortion – None in their Martch thorow [through] the countries shall waste, spoile or extorte [take by force] any Victuals [food] or Money, from any subject, upon pain of death.
Taking of Horses out of the Plow – No soldier shall take a horse out of a plough, or to wrong the Husbandmen [farmers], or cattel, or Goods, upon pain of death.

Duties in camp and garrison –
Swerving from the camp – No man shall depart a mile out of the Army or Camp without licence, [permission] upon pain of death.
Offering violence to Victuallers – No man shall do violence to any that brings Victuals to the camp, upon pain of death to whosoever shall in his quarter [the place where the soldiers lived], abuse, beat, fright his landlord, or any person else in the family, shall be proceeded against [treated as] as a Mutineer, and an enemy to Discipline.

Duties in Action –
Flying – No man shall abandon his colours, or flye away in Battail, upon pain of death.
Flinging away Arms – If a Pikeman throw away his pike, or a Musketeer his musket, he or they shall be punished with death.

⤴ SOURCE D: *There was a tough code of discipline in the New Model Army. These are some examples of their 'Lawes'.*

Work

1 Why did Parliament need a New Model Army?

  b Who was given the job of training the men?

  c According to Source D, what sort of men did Cromwell want fighting for him?

2 Look at Source D.

  a This list was made public and pinned up around England. Why do you think Cromwell did this?

  b Why do you think the New Model Army rules were so strict?

3 Was the New Model Army a success? Give a detailed answer.

4 Are you tough enough? Pretend you are a captain in the army and you have been given the job of talking to a group of men who have just joined up to fight. Prepare a one-minute speech about the rules in Cromwell's New Model Army.

—MISSION ACCOMPLISHED?—

• Do you know who improved Parliament's army?

• Can you name three rules that soldiers in the New Model Army had to follow?

• Could you explain how these rules helped them win the Civil War?

The Royalist armies lost the Civil War. England faced an uncertain future but nobody expected what happened next. At 2:00pm on 30 January 1649, King Charles Stuart – God's representative on earth, had his head chopped off! How did this happen? What had Charles done wrong? And who sentenced him to execution?

5: Why was Charles I executed?

MISSION OBJECTIVES

- To understand how and why the King of England was put on trial for his life.
- To know the key events of the trial.
- To be aware of how the judges arrived at their verdict.

In 1648, King Charles was kept as a prisoner in Carisbrook Castle on the Isle of Wight. In August, he secretly persuaded the Scots to invade England. They were helped out by those people who still supported Charles. The English Civil War was back on again. However, the second Civil War didn't last long because Royalist forces were easily beaten by Cromwell's New Model Army. Parliament had lost all faith in the King and met to discuss what to do with him. Out of 286 Members of Parliament, 240 thought Charles should be given another chance. However, when they next met for discussion, those same 240 members were stopped from entering Parliament by Cromwell's troops. This left 46 Members of Parliament to vote about what to do with the King.

By 26 votes to 20, it was decided that Charles should be put on trial for treason. A jury of 135 top lawyers and judges were chosen to try him. The trial was fixed for Saturday 20 January 1649 in Westminster Hall, London.

❚❚ PAUSE for Thought

How do Cromwell's actions compare to Charles'? Think about the actions of King Charles before the wars started.

The Trial

Day 1: Saturday 20 January 1649

Charles was brought to court by armed soldiers. A red velvet seat was placed for him to sit on. He refused to remove his hat but nobody forced him to. There were meant to be 135 judges but only 67 turned up.

❚❚ PAUSE for Thought

Only 67 judges turned up on the first day. The wife of one man who didn't show up shouted out, 'He has too much wit to be here' when his name was read out. What do you think she meant?

↵ SOURCE A: *A picture of the trial.*

First the charges were read out.

'Charles Stuart, King of England... traitorously waged a war against Parliament and the people. He renewed the war against Parliament in 1648. He is thus responsible for all the treasons, murders, rapings, burnings, damage and desolation caused during these wars. He is therefore a tyrant, traitor and murderer and an enemy to the commonwealth of England.'

↰ **SOURCE B:** *The crimes that Charles was charged with.*

▌▌PAUSE for Thought

Read Source B very carefully. Make sure you have understood what the charges mean. You might need to look up words such as 'desolation', 'tyrant' and 'commonwealth'. In your own words, write a short paragraph describing the charges made against Charles.

The man leading the trial, John Bradshaw, asked Charles to say whether he pleaded innocent or guilty to these charges. Charles laughed and refused to plead at all. He said:

'I would know by what power I am called here. I want to know by what authority, I mean lawful. There are many unlawful authorities in the world, thieves and robbers on the highway. Remember, I am your King, your lawful King. I have a trust committed to me by God, by old and lawful descent; I will not betray it to answer a new unlawful authority.'

↰ **SOURCE C:** *The King's response to the charges.*

▌▌PAUSE for Thought

Why do you think Charles uses the word 'lawful' so often? What do you think 'I have a trust committed to me by God' means? Throughout the trial, Charles refused to take his hat off, interrupted and even laughed at what was being said. Why do you think he behaved like this?

The day ended with Charles refusing to plead innocent or guilty – he even refused to accept that the court had any legal right to put him on trial.

Day 2: Monday 22 January

Seventy judges turned up on the second day. The court continued to ask Charles to plead innocent or guilty to the charges. Charles argued that the courts were the King's courts and under his authority – so how could the King be put on trial in his own court? At one point, Charles and Bradshaw appeared to argue with each other.

Bradshaw: Confess or deny the charge.
King: By what authority do you sit?
Bradshaw: We sit here by the authority of the commons of England and you are responsible to them.
King: I deny that! Show me one precedent.
Bradshaw: This is not to be debated by you.
King: The commons of England is not a Court of Law.
Bradshaw: It is not for prisoners to discuss.
King: Sir, I am not an ordinary prisoner.
Bradshaw: Take him away.

↰ **SOURCE D:** *The King and Bradshaw argued. Why did Bradshaw become so frustrated with Charles?*

↰ **SOURCE E:** *Bradshaw wore this metal-lined hat during the trial. Why do you think he did this?*

Work

It is 1649 and you have managed to get a seat in the gallery to watch the trial of Charles I. Write a short letter to a friend about the events of days one and two.

IMPORTANT: Choose whether you are either a supporter of Charles (a Royalist) OR a supporter of Parliament. Your letter should reflect your feelings. For example, a supporter of Charles might think his refusal to take his hat off was brave and courageous. Someone against him would think this was disrespectful to the judges.

Day 3: Tuesday 23 January

Seventy-one judges turned up on the third day. Once again, Charles refused to plead. He said that the court, which was chosen by the army, relied on force, not the law. He added, 'How I came here I know not, there is no law to make your King your prisoner.' Charles was taken away again after just a few minutes in court.

▮▮ PAUSE for Thought

Look at the first three days of the trial. In your opinion, is the trial going better for the King or his enemies?

Days 4–6: 24–26 January

Things weren't going as Parliament and Cromwell had hoped. Algernon Sydney, a leading judge, who refused to take part in the trial, said publicly, 'Firstly, the King cannot be tried by any court and secondly, no man should be tried in this court.'

The judges met without Charles for the next few days. They decided to write down a plea of 'guilty' despite the fact that Charles had chosen not to answer any of their questions properly. Finally, witnesses were heard.

Witness No. 1:

'I saw Charles stick his banner in the ground in Nottingham in 1642. This officially started the war. The war was Charles' fault then.'

Witness No. 2:

'King Charles once saw some of Parliament's troops being badly treated by Royalists. He said, "I do not care if they cut them three times more, for they are mine enemies." '

Later that day, the judges made their decision. They decided that Charles was guilty of all charges and called him to see them the next day.

Verdict and Sentence

Day 7: Saturday 27 January

Sixty-eight judges were there on the final day. Charles entered the hall (with his hat on) and sat on his chair. Then John Bradshaw read out the verdict. Bradshaw said that it was the duty of any king to talk with Parliament frequently. Charles hadn't done this and so had failed in his duties as a king. This started the war. At this point, Charles tried to make a statement but wasn't allowed to do so.

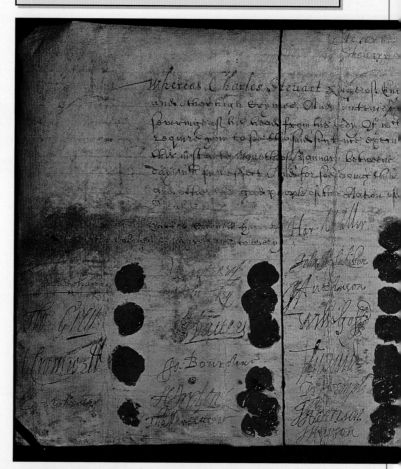

Witness No. 3:

'Here is a letter from King Charles to his son. He is asking his son to get a foreign army together to invade England. Charles wants foreigners to kill Englishmen. He can't be trusted... he's a traitor.'

> 'This court does judge that Charles Stuart as a tyrant, traitor, murderer and a public enemy, shall be put to death by the severing of his head from his body.'

SOURCE D: *The death sentence passed on King Charles.*

The execution date was set for Tuesday 30 January. The **death warrant** was signed by 59 judges… who then went off to pray!

> 'I tell you, we will cut off his head with the crown upon it.'

SOURCE E: *Oliver Cromwell speaking in January 1649.*

SOURCE F: *Charles I's death warrant. Forty men signed it straight away but others had to be forced to sign it.*

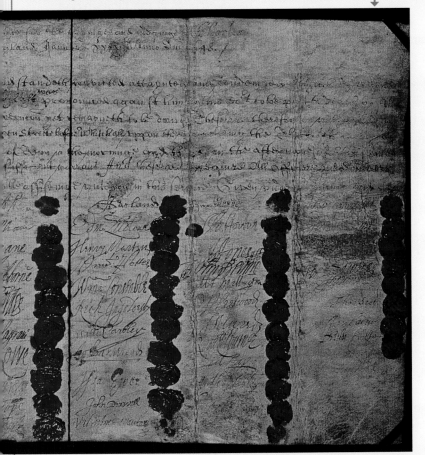

Hungry for MORE

Why not write a short script for, and perform, a role-play about the trial of King Charles? In groups, take on the roles of Charles, Bradshaw, the spectators and the judges. You will also need a narrator to tell the story of the trial.

WISE-UP Words

death warrant
execution
revolution

▌▌ PAUSE for Thought

- Look at the death warrant carefully. Can you make out any of the names? Look for Oliver Cromwell's signature.
- Look at Sources E and G. Write a sentence or two describing Cromwell's attitude to the trial.
- Only 59 judges signed the death warrant. Look again at page 98 and find out how many people were first chosen to make up the jury. What does this tell you?
- Look up the word 'revolution' in a dictionary. Is this a suitable word to describe the events of 20–27 January 1649?

> 'He is come, he is come and now we are doing the great work that the whole nation will be full of.'

SOURCE G: *Said by Oliver Cromwell after seeing King Charles walk to court on the final day.*

Work

Write another letter to your friend (or continue with your letter from the previous page), about the events of days three to seven. This time you will have to include your opinion of the verdict. Remember, you are writing as a supporter of Parliament or of Charles.

MISSION ACCOMPLISHED?

- Can you explain how Cromwell managed to put Charles on trial?
- Do you know what Bradshaw and the King argued about?
- Could you tell somebody what Charles was found guilty of and the punishment he faced?

We all know that there weren't any televisions at this time. There were no six o'clock news programmes, no newsflashes and certainly no special live reports. However, if there were, the events of Tuesday 30 January 1649 might have been presented like this…

6: Charlie for the chop!

—————— **MISSION OBJECTIVES** ——————

- To understand how Charles spent the last few hours of his life.
- To know the details of his execution.
- To be aware of how people reacted to the King's death.

TV Presenter: We are very sorry to interrupt your Tuesday afternoon film but the news we have been expecting has just been confirmed. Charles Stuart, King of England, is dead. Shortly after 2:00pm, he was beheaded outside Whitehall Banqueting House, London. Over to Annette Ball, our live reporter at the scene.

Live Reporter: Thank you Fiona, amazing scenes here in London today. The execution was planned for around 12 noon, so early this morning the King went for a walk through St James' Park with his pet spaniel, Rogue. He ate some bread, drank some red wine and then insisted on putting on two shirts before he started his final journey.

TV Presenter: Why two shirts, Annette?

Live Reporter: It's very chilly here today in London, Fiona, and apparently Charles didn't want to start shivering from the cold. He didn't want the public to think that he was trembling with fear.

TV Presenter: You say that they planned to execute him at 12 noon but he was killed shortly after 2:00pm. Why the delay?

Live Reporter: Firstly, the usual executioner refused to do it. Then 38 other men were each offered £100 to do it. One by one they refused. Eventually, two men agreed to do it in disguise. They wore masks, wigs and false beards.

TV Presenter: So what happened next?

Live Reporter: The King arrived shortly before 2:00pm. He stepped out onto the black cloth-covered scaffold, took off his jewels and his cloak, and then tucked his hair into a cap. He spoke calmly to those men near to him, kneeled down to pray and then put his head on the block.

TV Presenter: Was it a clean cut, Annette?

Live Reporter: Yes it was, Fiona. One clean chop. Then one of the axemen held up Charles' head for all to see. One eyewitness told me, 'There was such a groan by the thousands then present, as I never heard before and desire I may never hear again.'

TV Presenter: Describe the scene now, Annette.

Live Reporter: The King has just been taken away in a wooden coffin. Now people are paying to dip their handkerchiefs in the King's blood. Others are trying to break off pieces of the scaffold covered in his blood. Some of the soldiers guarding the scaffold will make a fortune today! Incredible scenes, Fiona. What can the country expect next? Back to you in the studio…'

TV Presenter: That's the big question tonight. King Charles is dead… so what happens now? What will Parliament do?

That must have been the question on everyone's lips. With no king, what sort of job would Parliament do?

↵ **SOURCE A:** *A drawing of the execution, drawn straight after the event.*

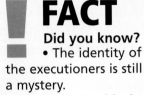 **FACT**

Did you know?
• The identity of the executioners is still a mystery.
• The execution block was 45cm long and 15cm wide. There was also special equipment to harness the King if he refused to put his head on the block.
• The King's head was sewn back on and he was quietly buried in Windsor Castle. In 1813, a doctor stole one of the King's neck bones and used it to hold salt at dinner parties. Queen Victoria wasn't amused and ordered him to put it back.

↵ **SOURCE B:** *A painting of the execution, painted soon after the event.*

Work

1 a Why do you think so many people refused to execute Charles? Give as many reasons as you can.

b Why did the two men finally agree to do it?

c Think carefully. Why did the executioners insist that Charles tuck his long hair into a cap?

2 Look at Source A. What is wrong with this print? Your answer to 1b might give you a clue.

3 a Look at Source B. You will notice four smaller pictures surrounding the main one. Describe what you think each of the smaller pictures shows.

b Why do you think that the woman in the main picture has fainted?

c Why do you think some people wanted to dip their handkerchiefs in the dead king's blood?

4 Many people didn't want Charles to die. Look back over pages 98–103 and write down as many examples as you can to show this.

5 Design a front page for a newspaper reporting the amazing events of Tuesday 30 January 1649. Try to do the following:
• Write a version that favours the supporters of the King, or those who decided to execute him.

• Show your report to a classmate and see if he or she can spot the parts of writing that show **bias**.

— MISSION ACCOMPLISHED? —

• Could you tell somebody about how Charles spent the morning of Tuesday 30 January 1649?
• Do you know what happened to him in the afternoon?
• Can you explain how some people reacted?

HOW TOLERANT WAS CROMWELL'S COMMONWEALTH?

More than any other figure in British history, Oliver Cromwell divides opinion. To some, he was a great man who improved and changed the way Britain was run, making it a safer, stronger and fairer place to live. To others, he was an intolerant, power-hungry monster who murdered and persecuted throughout his time as Lord Protector. Over the next eight pages, we are going to look at some of the things that have affected Cromwell's reputation and you are going to decide just how tolerant Cromwell's Commonwealth was.

1: Cromwell: the modern man?

MISSION OBJECTIVES

- To understand why people admired and respected Cromwell.
- To understand why people disliked Cromwell.
- To identify examples of Cromwell being tolerant and intolerant.
- To form your own opinion of Oliver Cromwell.

Look at the picture of the statue. The figure holding the Bible and the sword is Oliver Cromwell. The statue is right outside the Houses of Parliament. Apart from Queen Victoria, more streets in Britain are named after Cromwell than any other ruler and in a 2002 BBC survey of the British public, he was voted the 10th Greatest Briton of all time. So why did somebody think he deserved a statue outside the most important building in Britain? Why has he got so many roads named after him? And why do many people today think Cromwell was a great man?

↵ SOURCE A: *Photograph of Cromwell's statue in Westminster.*

'I'm a monarchist [someone who thinks Britain should have a monarch] but I believe the greatest Briton ever was Oliver Cromwell, a Republican revolutionary who killed the King. Why? Because he was an ordinary man with a passion for this country. When Britain stood on the edge of anarchy he emerged from obscurity to help give us Parliamentary democracy – our proudest ever achievement. Not bad for a farmer.'

↖ SOURCE B: *Historian Professor Richard Holmes on BBC's 'Great Britons' television programme, 2002.*

Look at the boxes covering the different aspects of Cromwell's character and how tolerant his Commonwealth was. Before you start, make sure you know what the word 'tolerant' means.

Cromwell the Fair
Cromwell is often praised for cutting out a lot of **corruption** in England. It became far more difficult to buy or **bribe** your way out of trouble under the Commonwealth and the fact that you came from a rich family no longer meant you could escape the law. Just look at what happened to Charles!

Cromwell the Soldier
It was Cromwell who created Britain's first full-time, permanent army. Before the Commonwealth, armies dealt with emergencies, like an invasion or rebellion, and then all the soldiers were sent back to their old jobs when the problem had passed. The 30 000 soldiers in Cromwell's army made England far stronger and safer from invasion, and Cromwell was both feared and respected by France and Spain.

Cromwell the Popular Republican
To some, Cromwell was a man of the people; a man who rose from being a lowly farmer with no experience as a soldier, into being the man who saved a nation from a cruel and intolerant king. He had Charles' head chopped off, after all, and throughout history many have thought that a country without a monarch is a fairer country. People who believe this are known as Republicans.

Cromwell the Liberal
When Charles was in charge, a lot of things that he disagreed with were **censored** (banned). This was not the case under Cromwell and there was an explosion of people publishing their ideas and books. For the first time, large numbers of women were able to have their work published and read. Some believed that the position and opportunities of women also improved under the Commonwealth. Cromwell himself had many female friends, something no other male ruler of England had ever done. He continued to live with his wife Elizabeth when he moved into royal apartments, breaking centuries of tradition. Up to that point, the ruler of England was not expected to actually live with his wife!

Cromwell the Democrat
Others admire Cromwell because they believe he modernized and improved the country. Under Cromwell's Commonwealth, Parliament was given more power than it had ever had in its history and the way it was elected was made much fairer.

'At dinner we talked much of Cromwell, all saying he was a brave fellow and did owe the crown he got to himself.'

⤷ **SOURCE C:** *From 'The Diary of Samuel Pepys', 8th February 1667.*

❚❚ PAUSE for Thought
Queen Victoria may have more streets named after her than any other ruler but more books have been written about Oliver Cromwell than any of the monarchs. As you read through this enquiry, see if you can work out why that is.

Work ⟞‿‿‿.
Imagine you've been asked to write the words for a plaque that will appear on Cromwell's statue. You are allowed to use no more than 100 words. Make sure you mention lots of different reasons why Cromwell has been admired over the years. You might want to include some quotes from Sources B and C.

——— MISSION ACCOMPLISHED? ———
- Can you explain three reasons why people admire Cromwell?
- Have you written a fitting inscription for his statue?

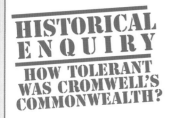
There are no statues of Cromwell in Ireland. In fact, when the Irish Prime Minister visited an important British politician in the 1990's, he marched straight back out of his office as soon as he had arrived. When asked why he had left, the Irish PM said, 'I'm not coming in until you take down the picture of that murdering…!' He was talking about the portrait of Oliver Cromwell that hung over the mantlepiece. So why are Irish interpretations of Cromwell so very different from those in Britain? Just what did he do to become so hated in Ireland? And does he deserve his terrible reputation there?

2: Cromwell: the curse of Ireland

MISSION OBJECTIVES
- To understand how Cromwell is viewed in Ireland.
- To understand what he did to earn his reputation in Ireland.
- To decide if he deserves his terrible reputation.

English rulers had been interfering in what was going on in Ireland since the 1100s. Many English kings had tried to rule Ireland but all had failed. Henry VIII called himself the King of Ireland but had never even visited!

Some Tudor monarchs thought they had a better chance of controlling Ireland if they sent English people to live there. As you can imagine, the Irish weren't very happy with foreigners turning up and taking their best land. Many rebelled against the new landowners and, every time they did, the rebel leaders had their land taken off them and given to Englishmen. As more and more English **settlers** moved to Ireland, relations between the two groups got worse and worse.

By 1640, over 25 000 Englishmen (and many Scots) had gone to live in Ireland. The settlers were Protestants whilst the Irish remained Catholic. In 1641, the hatred between the two groups burst out into violence and the Irish killed thousands of English and Scottish settlers. The English wanted revenge, but for a while they were distracted by the English Civil War and were unable to resolve the Irish question.

Cromwell and Ireland
Irish Catholics supported Charles I during the English Civil War. When Charles lost his head, the Irish still supported his son, the future Charles II. England's new leader, Oliver Cromwell, decided to sort out the Irish once and for all and took an army of 12 000 men with him, landing in Ireland in August 1649. Look at the seventeenth-century rules of warfare and then read through the cartoon of Cromwell's actions at Drogheda.

Seventeenth century rules of war! A **besieged** city that refuses an opportunity to surrender and is then taken by attack can expect no **mercy**!

1. Cromwell took his army to the coastal town of Drogheda. He gave the Royalists inside the town the opportunity to surrender.

2. The town was very well protected with a 20-foot-high wall and 29 huge guard towers. The Royalist defenders were so confident they could keep Cromwell out that their leader, Sir Arthur Aston, said, 'He who could take Drogheda, could take Hell.' Cromwell's offer was turned down.

5. Growing furious and desperate, Cromwell personally led the third attack on the hole. His men finally broke inside the town, and Cromwell ordered that no armed man or Catholic priest be left alive!

6. Cromwell's men swept through the town, slashing down holy men as if they were soldiers. Sir Arthur Aston was **bludgeoned** to death with his own wooden leg after rumours had spread that it was full of gold coins!

SOURCE A: *This is what Cromwell said to Parliament when asked about the massacre.* ↴

'The righteous judgement of God on these barbarous wretches who have imbued [covered] their hands with so much innocent blood.'

SOURCE B: *Words from the song 'Young Ned of the Hill', released by Irish musicians The Pogues in 1989.* ↱

'A curse upon you Oliver Cromwell, you who raped our motherland, I hope you're rotting down in Hell for the horrors that you sent.'

'So that spilling of blood may be prevented, I thought it right to summon you to surrender this place. If this is refused, you will have no cause to blame me.'

↱ **SOURCE C:** *Letter written by Cromwell to Sir Arthur Aston, in command of the Royalist soldiers in Drogheda. The rules of war at the time meant that if an enemy is given the chance to surrender and doesn't take it, they can later be killed if caught. If they do surrender, it would be wrong to kill them.*

WISE UP Words

besieged
bludgeon
mercy
settlers

✚ Hungry for MORE

Do you think there should be rules for wars, like in a football match? After all, the idea of a war is to kill each other isn't it? There are still rules for wars that take place today. This set of rules is known as the Geneva Convention. See if you can find out what these rules are and decide if you agree with them.

Work

1 a Imagine you are a soldier in Cromwell's army. You are totally loyal to your leader and support his actions in Ireland. Write a letter home to your family explaining why you were in Ireland and what you have been doing.

b Now write another letter. This time imagine you are an Irish Catholic who lived in Drogheda and managed to survive the events of 1649. Explain what happened and how people feel about Cromwell.

c In what ways are your two letters similar, and in what ways are they different? Give reasons for you answer.

2 How useful is Source B to an historian investigating modern attitudes to Cromwell in Ireland?

3 Do you think Cromwell deserves his reputation in Ireland? Explain your answer carefully.

___ **MISSION ACCOMPLISHED?** ___

• Have you decided whether Cromwell deserves his reputation in Ireland?

3. Cromwell immediately ordered his huge siege guns to fire at the town. By the following morning, a hole had been blown through the solid stone wall.

4. Cromwell sent his troops to attack the hole in the wall. The hole was too small for the cavalry to get through and the infantry were beaten back by fierce Irish resistance. Cromwell grew mad with frustration!

7. A church containing 300 of Drogheda's defenders was set on fire and they were burned alive. Around 3500 people died in Drogheda, with many survivors being sold into slavery and transported to Barbados. Just 150 of Cromwell's troops died.

8. Cromwell then moved his army south and attacked the town of Wexford where another 2000 defenders, priests and civilians were killed. Over the next ten years, around a third of the entire Irish population were either killed, died of starvation or were sold into slavery. Nearly all land in Ireland owned by Catholics was taken off them and given to English and Scottish Protestants.

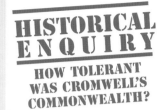
Cromwell allowed Jews to live in England for the first time in 365 years. Under the Commonwealth, Jews were free to build synagogues, celebrate religious festivals and live and work openly as people who didn't believe that Jesus was the son of God. But why were Jews banned from England in the first place? Just why did Cromwell allow them back in? And does their return prove that Cromwell's Commonwealth was a tolerant place?

3: The return of the Jews!

MISSION OBJECTIVES

- To understand why the Jews were banned from England in the first place.
- To be aware of the reasons why they were allowed to return under the Commonwealth.
- To decide if the return of the Jews proves that the Commonwealth was a tolerant place.

Large numbers of Jews first came to Britain with William the Conqueror in 1066. Under the laws of their religion, Jews were able to lend people money; something the Church banned Christians from doing. William thought that this would be useful in making his new country richer and stronger. Unfortunately for the Jews, being the people that everyone owed money to didn't make them very popular. Some people thought it would be easier, and cheaper, to just murder the Jews rather than pay them back. Just like in the rest of Europe, Jews were **persecuted** all over England until finally, in 1290, Edward I expelled all Jews from the country.

For the next 365 years, it was illegal for any Jew to live in England. Things began to change when a Portuguese **Rabbi** (Jewish priest), who was living in Holland, wrote to Oliver Cromwell asking for Jews to be readmitted. Cromwell met with Rabbi Menasseh ben Israel in 1656 to listen to his arguments and decided to organise a committee of politicians, businessmen and judges to decide what to do. The 'Whitehall Conference' argued for over two weeks.

A Puritan

A businessman

In the Bible it says that the Jews must be **converted** to Christianity before the Second Coming of Jesus can happen. We must let the Jews into England so we can turn them to our faith and allow Christ to return!

Many Jews have become very rich in Amsterdam trading with people in the West Indies, North America and Asia. If we let them move to London, we can use their contacts and skills to make England richer and more powerful!

! FACT Our oldest ethnic minority

Jews have formed a successful and important part of British society ever since 1656. During commemorations of 350 years of British Jews in 2006, the Prime Minister Tony Blair said that the Jewish people were Britain's oldest ethnic minority and that society would be unimaginable without them. Famous British Jews include Benjamin Disreali, one of Britain's most successful and admired Prime Ministers. Some British Jews became very successful businessmen, such as Michael Marks, who co-founded Marks and Spencer, and Sir Alan Sugar. Many British Jews have been successful in show business, becoming some of Britain's biggest ever stars. These include Elizabeth Taylor, Orlando Bloom, Sid James and Joan Collins on the big screen and Peter Sellers, Sacha Baron Cohen and Matt Lucas in the world of comedy. Many Jews have fought and died for Britain in the wars since 1656, including Siegfried Sassoon, and six British Jews have received the Victoria Cross, the highest award for bravery, while serving their country.

A judge

Spain and Portugal have just kicked the Jews out of their countries. If we let them move to England they can tell us information about how strong those countries are and what they are planning to do. They will make perfect spies for us!

Another Puritan

The Jews are evil people who don't believe in our saviour Jesus Christ! We cannot let them spread their lies in England. They are just out for themselves and will cause nothing but hatred and trouble!

Work

1 Explain what is meant by the following words:
- synagogue;
- convert;
- persecute;
- Rabbi.

2 Explain why Jews were persecuted and banned from England.

3 Look at the reasons that people gave for letting the Jews return to England during the Whitehall Conference. Write a couple of sentences explaining how people thought that the Jews would:
- make England richer?
- help England against her rivals?
- be useful to Christians?

The Whitehall Conference just couldn't decide what to do. Cromwell was not won over by the argument to keep the Jews out and mocked those who preached hatred against them. But not even Cromwell could get everybody to agree to allow the Jews to return. In the end, Cromwell made the decision himself and said that the old law banning Jews was out of date – and let them back in. By the end of the 1650's, there were **synagogues** and Jewish Cemeteries in London. They have been there ever since!

—— MISSION ACCOMPLISHED? ——

- Could you explain why Jews were banned from England in the first place?
- Can you name two reasons why some people wanted them to return during the Commonwealth?
- Have you decided whether this proves that the Commonwealth was a tolerant place?

We already know that Cromwell's Commonwealth tolerated some different religions. He was a strict Protestant himself, so he allowed Protestant churches to pop up all over the country – and we have just studied the fact that he allowed the Jews to return to England. But in 1656, a man called James Nayler and his friends staged a demonstration that tested just how tolerant the Commonwealth was… and I bet he wished he hadn't bothered!

4: The strange case of James Nayler

MISSION OBJECTIVES

- To be able to explain how and why James Nayler was punished.
- To decide if his case proves that the Commonwealth was a tolerant place.

Nayler was a leading member of a Protestant group known as the Quakers or the Society of Friends. Quakers believed that there was no need for priests or vicars in order to get in touch with God. They believed that all humans had an equal share of the 'inner light' of Jesus, and Nayler decided to show people exactly what he meant, with disastrous consequences!

Nayler's group decided to re-enact Jesus' arrival in Jerusalem on Palm Sunday. Jesus is said to have ridden into Jerusalem on a donkey as people threw palm leaves in his path while shouting 'hosanna'. In Nayler's case, he entered the city of Bristol on a horse, as his followers threw clothes and rags in his muddy path while shouting 'holy, holy, holy'.

Nayler's 'crime'

Nayler enters Bristol, intending to show people that the spirit of Jesus was in everybody. He was accused of impersonating Jesus and charged with blasphemy.

The people of Bristol were horrified by Nayler's actions. The Quakers that lived in the city were quick to say that the demonstration had nothing to do with them! Nayler was accused of 'claiming to be the equal of Christ' and of creating his own band of disciples. He was charged with **blasphemy**!

The case caused such a sensation that people in London soon heard about it. In Parliament, some politicians were saying that religious tolerance had gone too far – and they needed to get a bit tougher! They summoned Nayler to London and told him he would stand trial for his life. They completely ignored the fact that Britain had a Judge and Jury system and decided to try the case themselves.

Parliament very quickly found Nayler guilty of blasphemy but argued fiercely over how he should be punished. Some demanded that Nayler should be stoned to death for what he had done. Others, including Oliver Cromwell, questioned whether Parliament should be involved at all and asked it to be **lenient**. Eventually, a compromise was reached.

❚❚ PAUSE for Thought

Have you studied any figures in your history lessons that were less tolerant than Cromwell?

Nayler's punishment

The first part of Nayler's punishment was to be whipped through the streets of London.

He was then placed in the pillory.

Nayler then had a red hot iron stabbed through his tongue!

Next, he had the letter 'B' (standing for 'blasphemer') burned into the middle of his forehead.

He was then taken back to Bristol and made to repeat his ride in reverse, while facing his horse's bottom, before being put in prison for two years hard labour.

▌▌ PAUSE for Thought

Now that you have studied the Commonwealth, do you think Cromwell deserves a statue outside the Houses of Parliament? Explain your answer.

What about the Catholics?

The only religious group that Cromwell really picked on were the Catholics. He ordered the execution of Catholic priests in Ireland remember and, back in England, life became tough for Catholics in the Commonwealth.

Work _____

Answer the following questions:

a Who were the Quakers?

b Describe Nayler's entry into Bristol.

c Why do you think people were offended by Nayler's entry?

d What is meant by the word 'blasphemy'?

e Why was Nayler asked to go to Parliament?

f In what ways did parliament disagree over Nayler's punishment?

g In the end, how was Nayler punished?

h What is your opinion of Nayler's punishment?

—— MISSION ACCOMPLISHED? ——

• Could you explain to somebody how and why James Nayler was punished?

• Have you decided if the Commonwealth was tolerant towards him?

Whatever happened to Cromwell's head?

MISSION OBJECTIVES

- To understand who controlled England after Cromwell's death.
- To know the strange story about Cromwell's head.

Oliver Cromwell, Lord Protector, died of malaria in September 1658. John Evelyn wrote in his diary 'November 22nd 1658: It was the joyfulest funeral I have ever saw, for there was none that cried but the dogs, which the soldiers hooted away with a barbarous nasty noise, drinking and taking tobacco on the streets as they went…'.

WARNING IT'S A VERY DISGUSTING TALE

▐▐ PAUSE for Thought

Sounds a bit strange, doesn't it? A 'joyful funeral' where no one cries! It seems that many people weren't too upset at Cromwell's funeral – why? How did some of the soldiers show their attitude towards Cromwell?

Cromwell was buried at Westminster Abbey and his son, Richard, was made Lord Protector. He didn't really want the job and would sooner have been left alone as a farmer. Unable to stop the arguing between Parliament and the army, Richard resigned after only a few months. After a few more months of confusion, a new Parliament asked Charles I's son to return from exile abroad to become King. By 1660, the republic was over and England and Wales had a new king. One of King Charles II's first actions was a brutal one – kill the men who killed his father.

▐▐ PAUSE for Thought

How many men signed Charles I's death warrant (you might have to look back a few pages)? In signing away King Charles' life, many had signed away their own!

Fifteen of the men who had signed Charles I's death warrant were already dead by 1660, including Cromwell and Judge Bradshaw. The King ordered their bodies to be dug up and hung from the gallows at Tyburn. Some others had escaped abroad to America, several were arrested but died in prison, but thirteen of the regicides (king killers) were executed.

So what about Cromwell's head?

1: 1658
Cromwell dies.
Doctor Bates cuts out and weighs his brain. He says it weighs 82.5 oz. The average brain weighs 49 ounces – Bates was probably lying. Why?

4: 1702
Barnes dies.
He tells his family where he has hidden the head. They sell it to a Frenchman who puts it in a museum.

CROMWELL'S HEAD 1658

5: 1738
Museum owner dies.
A young actor called Samuel Russell buys it. He pays his rent by charging people to see it.

7: 1814
Dr Wilkinson buys head. He keeps the head in a box, wrapped in silk. He writes that an ear is missing, there's a hole in the top where a pole has been and there are axe marks on the neck.

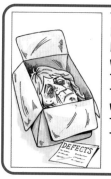

DEFECTS

SOURCE A: *Oliver Cromwell, painted in 1650. He told the artist, 'Do not flatter me at all, but show all the wrinkles, pimples and warts.'*

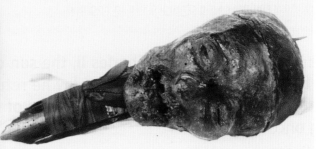

WISE-UP Words

gallows
malaria
regicide

SOURCE B: *A photo of the remains of Cromwell's head. You were told it was a disgusting tale!*

2: 1660
King Charles II wants to punish Cromwell.
Body dug up and hanged at Tyburn. His head was stuck on a pole outside Westminster Abbey.

3: 1685
Head stays on pole for 24 years.
Strong wind blows head off pole. It is found by a soldier called Barnes who takes it home and hides it in his chimney.

6: 1789
Russell sells head.
A group of businessmen buy the head for £230. It goes on display in Bond Street, London.

8: 1935
Doctor examines the head.
They decide that the man has definitely had his head cut off and that the pimples and warts do match Cromwell's portrait.

9: 1960
Wilkinson's family gives head away.
The head is given to Cromwell's old college, Sidney Sussex, in Cambridge. The head was buried secretly. It is still there today.

Work

1 a What does the word 'regicide' mean?

b Why do you think Charles II wanted to punish all the men involved in his father's death – even the ones who were already dead?

2 Read the story about Cromwell's head carefully.

a Why do you think soldier Barnes hid the head?

b Why do you think Dr Wilkinson was convinced that he had bought Cromwell's head?

c What evidence did the doctors have in 1935 that the head was Cromwell's?

d Why do you think the head was finally buried in secret?

e Today, experts know where Cromwell's head is buried but can they ever really be sure that it is actually Cromwell's head? Think carefully about your answer.

3 Prepare and act out a short role-play called 'The story of Cromwell's head':
- write out a script;
- take on some of the roles in the story, for example, Bates, Barnes, Russell;
- find a suitable 'head' (an old football perhaps);
- act it out in class.

MISSION ACCOMPLISHED?
- Can you what is meant by the term 'regicide'?
- Could you name three different places where Cromwell's head was kept?

The return of the king

MISSION OBJECTIVES

- To understand how, when and why England got itself a new king after Cromwell's death.
- To know how the new king changed life in England.

29 May 1660 was a special day for King Charles II, the son of executed Charles I. Firstly, it was his thirtieth birthday. Secondly, it was the day he returned to London after living abroad for almost ten years. Thousands lined the streets of Europe's largest city, London. England had a king once more.

Charles had been able to return to the throne because many people in Parliament believed that the republic had failed. Cromwell had behaved exactly like a king and bullied Parliament into getting his own way. His strict religious views meant that a lot of fun had been removed from people's lives – he even banned Christmas in 1652! By 1658, Lady Lucy Hutchinson, one of Cromwell's biggest supporters, wrote: 'The whole land has grown tired of him and his company of silly, mean fellows called Major Generals.' When Cromwell died later that year, his son Richard carried on running the country. By 1660, Parliament had had enough and, consequently, Charles II was asked to leave France and come home to London.

SOURCE B: *Coffee houses were very popular in London. In fact, by 1660, the three most common hot drinks were tea (from India), coffee (from Arabia) and cocoa (from Mexico). Melons, bananas and pineapples were available, although not many people bought fruit because they thought it caused diseases. Smoking tobacco in pipes was also very popular.* ↱

SOURCE A: *The magnificent procession in London which marked Charles II's coronation in 1660.* ↳

Charles was known as the 'Merry Monarch' because he liked to have fun. He brought back all the sports and entertainment that the Puritans had banned. The King himself could often be seen racing down the River Thames in a yacht, gambling on horses at Newmarket, visiting the theatre in Drury Lane or playing 'pell mell' (a kind of combined hockey/golf/croquet game) along Pall Mall. Cockfighting and bear-baiting were back… and the people of London loved him for it. In fact, the Merry Monarch's London was a very interesting place.

By 1660, London was the largest city in Europe. Nearly 500 000 people lived amongst its narrow, winding, cobbled-stoned streets. As the city had grown, new houses sprang up all over the place. The tall, wooden houses were tightly packed together – leaving little space for fresh air or sunlight to break through. In fact, in some cases, the top floors of houses on opposite sides of the street nearly touched each other.

During the day, London was a noisy, busy, hectic place packed full of people selling goods, running errands or enjoying one of the city's smoke shops or coffee houses.

At night, London could be extremely dangerous. Thieves and robbers lurked in dark alleys and drunken brawls were heard all night long. Conmen, beggars and prostitutes pestered people constantly and pickpockets stole from any unsuspecting citizen.

The streets were full of rubbish too – and open sewers ran through the middle of them. Rats and fleas were everywhere. There were no toilets as we know them, just a hole in the ground or a bucket that you emptied into the street when it got full. Water came from street pumps that took the water straight from the River Thames. All the filth from the street washed into the river. It would have been bad enough to wash your clothes in water from a pump in 1660, let alone drink it! It is little wonder that only one person in ten lived to the age of 40.

Nobody really understood the link between dirt and disease as we do today and, by 1665, London was one of the filthiest places in England. That summer was unusually hot, so the city must have been very smelly indeed. The hot, moist, filthy atmosphere was a perfect breeding ground for germs.

↰ SOURCE C: *A picture of London in 1616.*

↳ SOURCE D: *Wealthy people used these hand-held 'taxis' to get around as the streets were either too filthy – or too dangerous – to step out onto.*

Work

Imagine you lived in London in the weeks after Charles II had been restored as king. Write a letter to a friend in the country, describing the city at the time of the 'Merry Monarch'.

___**MISSION ACCOMPLISHED?**___

• Can you explain why Charles II might have been called the 'Merry Monarch'?

Bring out your dead!

_____ MISSION OBJECTIVES _____
• To understand what people knew about the spread of plague and disease in seventeenth-century London.

In 1603, a plague had killed 40 000 people; in 1609, 12 000, in 1625, 35 000 and in 1636, 10 000. This time it would kill even more. The plague was about to claim over 100 000 victims. A London gentleman called Samuel Pepys kept a diary during the worst outbreak of plague for hundreds of years. In it, he recorded the main events in London during that burning hot, plague-ridden summer of 1665.

7 June
'The hottest day that I have ever felt in my life. In Drury Lane I saw two or three houses were marked with a red cross and the words 'Lord have mercy upon us' written on the door. This worried me so much that I bought a roll of tobacco to smell and chew.'

17 June
'I was riding in a coach through the street when my driver suddenly stopped. He told me that he felt sick and could hardly see where he was going. I felt very sorry for him – did he have the plague?'

29 June
'I travelled on the river today and saw wagons full of people trying to leave the city. I sent my wife to stay with friends at Woolwich – but I will remain working in my office. I hear the church bells ring five or six times a day for a funeral.'

20 July
'Walked home past Radcliff, where I hear the sickness is scattered almost everywhere. 1089 people died of plague this week. I was given a bottle of plague water today.'

8 August
'Poor Will, the man who used to sell us ale, his wife and three children died, all of them on the same day. 6102 people died of plague this week, but I fear that the true number is nearer 10 000. The graveyards are so full that plague pits have been dug outside the city walls that take up to 400 bodies.'

31 August
'Fires were lit to keep the air clean. The Mayor said that all fit people should be indoors by 9:00pm, so the sick can exercise and have some fresh air at night. All dogs and cats are to be caught and killed. People are being paid to kill them. Even public entertainment has been stopped, there's no theatre, no sports and no games. Any houses containing plague victims have to be sealed up for 40 days.'

3 September
'I bought a new wig but I am afraid to wear it. It might have been made from the hair of a dead plague victim! Grass is growing in the empty streets and there are no longer boats on the river – even the King has left London!'

The Difeafes and Cafualties this Week

		hopoft.nme	11
		Infants	16
		Killed by a fall from the Belfrey at Alhallows the Great	1
		Kingfevil	2
		Lethargy	1
		Palfie	1
		Plague	7165
Abortive	5	Rickets	17
Aged	43	Rifing of the Lights	11
Ague	2	Scowring	5
Apoplexie	1	Scurvy	2
Bleeding	2	Spleen	1
Burnt in his Bed by a Candle at St.Giles Cripplegate	1	Spotted Feaver	101
		Stilborn	17
Canker	1	Stone	2
Childbed	42	Stopping of the ftomach	9
Chrifomes	18	Strangury	1
Confumption	134	Suddenly	1
Convulfion	64	Surfeit	49
Cough	2	Teeth	121
Droplie	33	Thruth	5
Feaver	309	Timpany	1
Flox and Small-pox	5	Tiffick	11
Frighted	3	Vomiting	3
Gowt	1	Winde	3
Grief	3	Wormes	15
Griping in the Guts	51		
Jaundies	5		

Christned { Males — 95, Females — 81, In all — 176 } Buried { Males — 4095, Females — 4202, In all — 8297 } Plague — 7165

Increased in the Burials this Week ———— 607
Parishes clear of the Plague —— 4   Parishes Infected ———— 126

The afsize of Bread fet forth by Order of the Lord Mator and Court of Aldermen. A penny Wheaten Loaf to contain Nine Ounces and a half, and three half-penny White Loaves the like weight.

SOURCE A: *Searchers would check each dead body to work out the cause of death. Each week the number of dead and their cause of death were written on a Bill of Mortality. This one covers 12–19 September 1665.*

SOURCE B: *Some plague doctors would dress like this when visiting people with the plague.*

Leather hat
Mask with glass visor, beak stuffed with perfume or spice to avoid bad air
Stick for protection
Leather gloves to avoid handling the sick
Long leather coat

People still didn't know what caused the plague. Some thought it was caused by the position of the planets but most people thought it was caught by touching someone or from bad smells – and there were plenty of bad smells in London in 1665! Others thought it was sent by God as a punishment or it was spread by cats and dogs. Source B shows that some doctors took no chances.

! FACT
And so to bed
Samuel Pepys wrote his diary between 1660 and 1669. He wrote in **shorthand**, a type of coded writing that uses symbols and shortened words that can be written quickly. For years, nobody could work out the codes. Then in 1818, the code was broken by John Smith, who published the Pepys diary in 1825. In 1952, the stories from the diary were made into a musical called 'And so to bed' – the title came from the words Pepys used to end his diary each day.

WISE-UP Words
Bill of Mortality
searcher
shorthand

Work

1 Write a sentence or two to explain each of the following:
   Bill of Mortality • searchers

2 Read the diary again carefully and answer the following questions:
   a What do you think the red crosses and the writing on people's doors meant?
   b Why do you think Samuel Pepys bought a roll of tobacco to smell and chew?
   c How might the plague spread around the country?
   d What do you think 'plague water' was?
   e How did the Mayor try to deal with the plague? What do you think his reasons were for doing these things?

3 Look at Source A and then answer the following questions.
   a How many people died of the plague?
   b How many people died and were buried 'in all' during this week?
   c Work out what percentage of people were killed by the plague during this week? Your teacher will help you to do this.
   d What do you think is meant by: 'aged', 'grief', 'suddenly', and 'teeth' as causes of death?

MISSION ACCOMPLISHED?
• Can you list three things that London's Mayor did in an attempt to combat the spread of plague?
• Can you explain why a plague doctor wore his unique outfit?

Another nasty nursery rhyme

MISSION OBJECTIVES

- To understand the symptoms of the Great Plague.
- To know how a nursery rhyme tells us how people tried to avoid catching it.

There are different kinds of plague, each with a different cause. Historians cannot quite agree on the type of plague that hit London in 1665 but most think it was the bubonic plague. It gets its name from the 'buboes', or huge round boils which appeared in a victim's armpit or groin. There were lots of other nasty symptoms too, as you'll see later.

In 1665, people didn't understand what caused the plague or how to treat it properly. Today, we know most of the answers. We know that the plague was a germ that lived in the guts of fleas. These fleas were carried in the fur of the black rat. A single flea bite led to the plague and usually killed the victim.

Historians think that plague-infected rats and fleas brought the disease to England aboard boats bringing goods from Holland. Rats and fleas soon carried the disease all around the filthy streets of London. Towns such as Sunderland, Newcastle and Southampton were also hit by the plague, carried there by people escaping from London and by trading ships. By December, the plague was over but just as Londoners were recovering from one disaster, another was about to strike.

You will almost certainly have heard or even sung the following nursery rhyme. However, you probably didn't realise how nasty it was when you sang it!

As well as the pus filled buboes in the victim's armpit and groin, a circular rash of red and black spots appeared all over the body. Some people thought that the rash looked like a red rose. It was common to hear people ask, 'Can you see the mark of a rose on my body yet?' In other words, they wanted to know if they had the rash yet.

Ring a ring o' roses,

A pocket full of posies.

A-tishoo, a-tishoo!

We all fall down.

A 'posy' is a bunch of flowers. People carried flowers, herbs and spices to make the air around them smell sweeter. Why do you think they wanted to get rid of any bad smells?

Sneezing was one of the first symptoms of the plague. A high temperature, shivering, dizziness, vomiting and aches and pains would soon follow.

This line speaks for itself. In London alone, it is estimated that over 100 000 people died but historians can never be sure of the final number. Some deaths were never recorded as the plague because victims' families didn't want their houses sealed up. Thousands were secretly buried in gardens and fields.

Month	Number of deaths due to plague – recorded for London 1665
May	43
June	590
July	4117
August	19 046
September	26 219
October	14 373
November	3454
December	590

WISE-UP Words

bubonic
contemporary
symptoms

Hungry for MORE

There is a second verse to the 'Ring a ring o' roses' rhyme. Find out what it is and try to work out what each line means.

These are **contemporary** figures. This means that they are figures from the same period of time. In other words, they were added together in 1665.

Some people spent a fortune on crazy cures for the plague. It's easy to laugh at them now but try to imagine how scared the people must have felt in the summer of 1665. They were obviously willing to try anything!

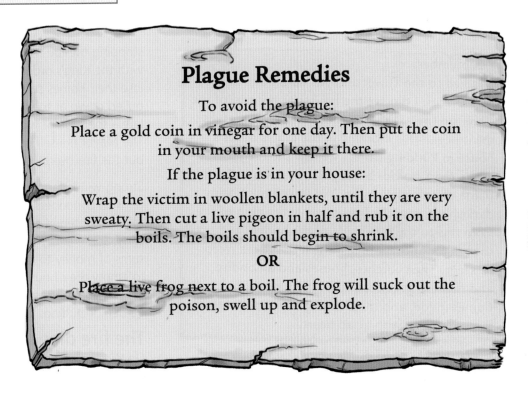

Plague Remedies

To avoid the plague:

Place a gold coin in vinegar for one day. Then put the coin in your mouth and keep it there.

If the plague is in your house:

Wrap the victim in woollen blankets, until they are very sweaty. Then cut a live pigeon in half and rub it on the boils. The boils should begin to shrink.

OR

Place a live frog next to a boil. The frog will suck out the poison, swell up and explode.

Work

1 a What caused the plague?

b Write down at least five symptoms.

2 Today, we know how the plague was caused. Look back at Samuel Pepys' diary of 31 August on page 116. Might any of the Mayor's actions actually have worked in stopping the spread of disease? Explain your answer carefully.

3 a Using the figures in the chart, draw a bar chart to show the increase in the number of plague deaths in 1665. Remember to give your bar chart a title.

b According to your graph, how many people died between May and December?

c Today, historians estimate that 100 000 people died of the plague. Why do you think the figures from 1665 are different?

FACT Smoking in school… allowed!

The boys at Eton school in Surrey were punished if they didn't smoke tobacco. Can you think of any reason why a teacher would want their students to smoke?

MISSION ACCOMPLISHED?

• Can you explain the meaning of every line of the nursery rhyme Ring a Ring o' Roses?

Who started the Great Fire of London?

MISSION OBJECTIVES

- To describe how the Great Fire devastated London.
- To understand how and why interpretations about the cause of the Great Fire have changed since 1666.
- To know how London was rebuilt after 1666.

In 1666, a London gentlemen named Samuel Pepys (pronounced 'Peeps') was living in Seething Lane, not far from the Tower of London. At three o'clock in the morning on Sunday 2 September his maid woke him up to tell him about a fire that had started in the city. Pepys got up, looked out of his window and decided that the fire was too far away from him to get worried. So he went back to bed. When Pepys woke later that morning, he took the fire a lot more seriously (see Source A).

2 September:
'Walked to the Tower and got up on one of the high places. I did see the houses at the end of the street on fire... The lieutenant of the Tower tells me it began this morning in the King's baker's house in Pudding Lane... we saw the fire grow... in the most horrid, bloody flame, not like the fine flame of an ordinary fire. We stayed till it being darkish, we saw the fire as one entire arch of fire from this to the other side of the bridge, and up the hill for above a mile long. It made me weep to see it. The churches, houses and all on fire, and flaming at once, and a horrid noise the flames made, and the cracking of houses at their ruin. So home with a sad heart.'

↳ SOURCE A: *From Samuel Pepys' diary.*

As the day went on, the fire got worse and worse. At midday, 300 houses had been burned down and people were starting to panic. London's buildings were made of wood and the houses were packed close together, so the fire spread quickly – especially as the long, hot summer of 1666 had dried out the timber so it burned easily.

There was no fire brigade at that time either. Buckets of water and large metal syringes or 'squirts' were the best the city could offer to fight the fire (see Source B).

London's burning

By the evening, the King was so concerned that he ordered houses in the path of the fire to be pulled down. The idea was to create a 'fire break' to stop the fire spreading to more houses. But the man in charge of stopping the fire – the Mayor of London – was struggling with the King's orders. To start with, people didn't want to lose their homes so they only allowed their houses to be pulled down at the last moment. And by then it was too late – the piles of wood and plaster just caught fire too! The Mayor himself said, 'I have been pulling down houses, but the fire overtakes us faster than we can do it.'

Strong winds fanned the fire for the next few days – and terrified Londoners fled the city in fear. The streets were full of frightened people, loaded up with all they could carry. Some crafty horse and cart owners charged huge sums of money to desperate homeowners who were trying to empty their houses and take their possessions to safety. Samuel Pepys himself buried all of his valuables in his back garden, including: 'a large parmesan cheese'!

The fire dies down

On Wednesday, the King and his brother brought sailors in to blow up houses with gunpowder. The gaps created by the explosives stopped the fire spreading so quickly and by Thursday the fire was dying down. But the heart of Europe's largest city had been reduced to ashes – 130 000 houses and 88 churches had been destroyed. Around 100 000 people were made homeless. And then the rumours started – some were saying the fire wasn't an accident at all! So who started the Great Fire of London?

SOURCE B: *Fire fighting equipment from the 1660s.* ↱

A fire squirt
A leather bucket
A fire hook

Work

1 Here is a list of some events during the Great Fire. They're all mixed up. Write down the events in the correct chronological order:

- Londoners start to leave the city.
- The fire begins to die down.
- The King orders houses to be pulled down.
- Samuel Pepys looks at the fire and goes back to bed.
- The fire starts.
- Londoners start to panic.
- The King and his brother take control and blow up houses.

2 Look at Source B.

a Draw each piece of fire-fighting equipment.

b Next to each item, explain why it failed to help put out the fire.

3 a Why do you think the fire spread so quickly?

b How was it eventually stopped?

! **FACT** **A cheesy tale!**
With the fire fast approaching, Samuel Pepys rushed to save some of his precious belongings from the inferno by burying them in his garden – including a big piece of cheese.

↳ **SOURCE C:** *A dramatic painting of the fire, painted at the time. (The Great Fire of London in 1666 (oil on canvas), Verschuier, Lieve (1630-86), The Bridgeman Art Library/Museum of Fine Arts, Budapest, Hungary.)*

SOURCE D: *A map of London made soon after the fire. The white area is the part that was destroyed by fire. Look for:*
i) the plans for a new London;
ii) a picture of the fire. ↴

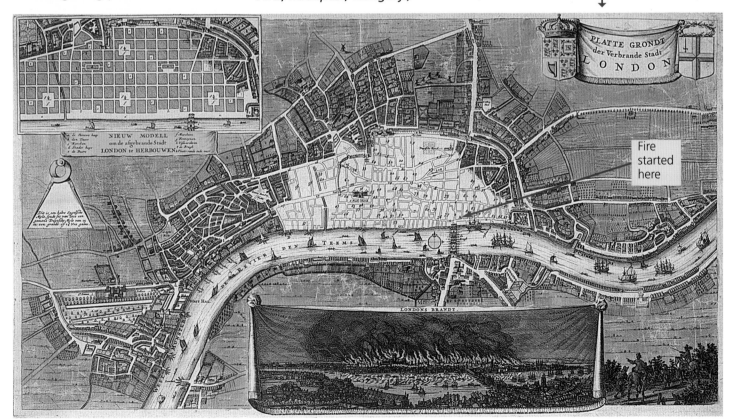

Fire started here

So how did the fire start?

The Great Fire of London was a disaster. One person at the time wrote, 'London is no more.' But many people at the time couldn't believe it was an accident. They suspected a plot. Was it the Catholics; perhaps even French Catholics?

In the days immediately after the fire had died down, rumours spread throughout the city and people were attacked at random. A Catholic was nearly beaten to death by a crowd who thought he was carrying fireballs (they were, in fact, tennis balls!). A French visitor was beaten up with an iron bar and another had his furniture smashed up by an angry mob. The mob thought they were both French spies!

Then, a week after the end of the fire, a Frenchmen living in London called Robert Hubert was arrested for using gunpowder to start the fire. He confessed and then offered to lead the investigation team to where he started the blaze. He was found guilty and hanged on 27 October 1666.

Historians today do not believe that Robert Hubert had anything to do with the fire. Many people at the time thought he did – after all, he was killed for starting it! Clearly opinions have changed over the past 300 years. So why, and how, are today's views about the start of the fire so different from the views of people in 1666?

⌐ SOURCE E: *The monument to the Great Fire. This 61 metre high column was built in 1669, near to the site of a baker's shop in Pudding Lane where the start of the fire had been traced to. An inscription carved into it at the time (since removed) says that the fire was caused by 'Catholics to introduce the Catholic religion and slavery'. Originally, the monument was to have a statue of King Charles II on top but the King refused. 'After all,' he said, 'I didn't start it'.*

'5 November: Sir Thomas Crew says, from what he has heard at the committee for investigating the burning of the city, that it was certainly done by a plot – it being proved that attempts were made in several places to increase the fire. Both in the city and in the country several Papists [Catholics] boasted that on such a day or in such a time we should find the hottest weather that ever was in England.'

⌐ SOURCE F: *From Samuel Pepys' diary.*

'Not many people died as a result of the Great Fire, but one of them was a Frenchman called Robert Hubert. He was found guilty of using gunpowder to start the fire and was hanged in October 1666. Too late, it was discovered that he wasn't even in England when the fire was started.'

⌐ SOURCE G: *From J. F. Aylett's 'In Search of History 1485–1714' (1984).*

'Robert Hubert, a London watchmaker who was born in France, was tried in October 1666 and executed on the 27th of that month. The only evidence against him was his own confession, which he later denied. It does not appear to be true that he was a Catholic, as he claimed. The fact that he was able to identify the site of the baker's house proved nothing since for a long time it had been on public show. He was in fact mentally disordered and had landed in London from Sweden two days after the fire had started.'

SOURCE H: *Robert Latham, a historian, writing in 1974.*

'The summer of 1666 was very hot... at the end of August and the beginning of September a strong easterly wind blew across the city of London drying the old wooden buildings... In the early hours of Sunday, 2 September, a fire broke out in a baker's shop not far from the Tower, and fanned by the strong winds, spread rapidly... Perhaps there was little that anyone could have done: the water pipes were of wood and in any case, the pumping house near London Bridge had been one of the first places to be destroyed... The flames roared along the tunnel-like alleys sweeping up the bone dry houses and exploding when they reached warehouses full of oil, tar, spirits and other inflammable materials. Near blazing churches, molten lead ran like water down the gutters.'

SOURCE I: *From Peter Moss' 'History Alive 1 1485–1714' (1980).*

'The fire started in the King's bakery run by Thomas Farynor in Pudding Lane. Farynor denied this at the time and a deluded French watchmaker called Robert Hubert claimed he did it. Although it was evident to judge and jury that he couldn't have done it, they hanged him anyway. His corpse was torn apart by an angry mob, suspecting a Popish [Catholic] plot. Justice wasn't done until 1986, when the Worshipful Company of Bakers [a kind of Baker's society] claimed official responsibility and apologised for the fire.'

SOURCE J: *From 'The Book of General Ignorance' by John Lloyd and John Mitchenson (2006).*

Work

Use all the evidence to help you to work out who started the Great Fire of London. Was it a Catholic or French plot, or simply an unfortunate accidental fire?

1 Find evidence of a plot.

Make notes on which sources support the theory that it was a plot to burn down London. Who could have done this? Which sources support the idea of a plot?

2 Find sources to suggest the fire was an accident.

Perhaps the fire was an accident? Make notes on the sources that support this idea. Where could the fire have started? Why did it spread so quickly? Write down your findings.

3 Think – which sources can you trust?

Can you rely on some sources more than others? Which sources might it be wrong to trust? Why do so many of the modern sources disagree with sources from the time of the fire? Why do you think Catholics were blamed by some people? Write down your opinions.

4 Time to reveal your findings.

Write a paragraph to explain how you think the Great Fire of London was started. Remember to back up your theories with the evidence provided!

What was so special about the Great Fire?

The Great Fire is important for a number of reasons. To start with, the fact that a French Catholic was hanged for starting the fire – and he wasn't even in the country when it began – shows how anti-Catholic and anti-French people were at the time. Catholics all over London were beaten up by angry mobs, indicating just how paranoid Londoners were about a 'Catholic takeover'. Also, the Great Fire is important because, to put it simply, it destroyed London.

Before the Great Fire, London was for the most part a filthy, stinking maze of streets and alleys full of dirt and disease. Fire destroyed five-sixths of the city and planning for the rebuilding of it began soon after the fire was finally out.

The King asked for plans for a new city and within two weeks an **architect** called Christopher Wren had written up his ideas. He planned a city with broad, straight streets, wide-open spaces and magnificent new brick or stone churches and homes.

New regulations for New London

- Building new homes out of wood is *BANNED*.
- All new houses should be built of *BRICK* or *STONE*.
- All new streets must be *WIDE*.
- Houses over 9m wide are only allowed on main streets.
- 100 existing streets must be *WIDENED*.
- The filthy Fleet River will be covered over and some new common **sewers** will be built.

↵ **SOURCE L:** *People would display a* **fire mark** *on the outside of their house to prove their insurance fees had been paid.*

❚❚ PAUSE for Thought

Why do you think Wren's plans for a new London included BROAD streets, WIDE-OPEN spaces and BRICK or STONE buildings?

↵ **SOURCE K:** *St Paul's Cathedral.*

Despite Wren's ideas for a magnificent new city, most of them were ignored. Homeless people wanted their homes built quickly and in exactly the same places as their old ones. Few people wanted to – or could afford to – give up their land to make London a nicer place to live. However, the King insisted on some changes.

By 1672, a new city had risen from the ashes. London looked like it had been planned properly – rows of houses, all the same height, made from the same building materials. Cleaner streets meant fewer rats and fleas. Stone buildings meant less chance of fire. Never again was there a plague or fire on the same scale as the ones of 1665 and 1666.

One of Wren's ideas that everyone loved was his plan for 51 new churches. The most famous, St Paul's Cathedral, took 35 years to build. By the time he died in 1723, Wren had been asked to build other magnificent buildings, including colleges and hospitals. Wren is buried in St Paul's. If you visit his grave, you will find the words 'Si Monumentum Requiris Circumspice' – they mean, 'If you seek his monument, look around you.'

❚ FACT
New London, new ideas

Insurance companies started up as a result of the Great Fire. Before, if your house burned down, you paid for it to be rebuilt. From 1666 onwards, a house owner could pay small sums of money to insure their property. If a fire started, the employees of the insurance company would put out the fire using their own fire engine.

Work ︵︵.

1 a How much of London was destroyed by the Great Fire?

b What sort of new city did Christopher Wren plan? Give reasons for his ideas.

c Why were all his plans not used?

d Do you think the inscription on Wren's grave is an appropriate one?

2 a Explain the phrase 'blessing in disguise'. You might like to discuss this with a classmate or a teacher.

b How might the Great Fire of London be seen as a blessing in disguise?

3 Look at Source L.

a What is insurance?

b Explain why insurance companies introduced fire marks?

──MISSION ACCOMPLISHED?──

• Can you explain how London changed as a result of the Great Fire?

What about the women?

- To understand how the lives of rich and poor women differed in the Tudor and Stuart periods.
- To be aware of how some men treated their wives.

Some of the most famous people in Tudor and Stuart history were women: Elizabeth I and Mary Queen of Scots, for example. But what about other women in general, everyday life? How were they treated? What was life like for them? Let's look for some answers.

Like poor men, poor women faced tough lives. In fact, their lives remained much the same as they had been for women in the Middle Ages. Almost 95% of the population still lived in the countryside and the women worked just as hard as the men.

'... get up, clean the clothes, milk the cows, collect eggs, feed the pigs, dress the children, prepare food, bake bread, brew ale, make butter and cheese, mend clothes, go to market, sell butter, cheese and eggs...'

SOURCE A: *A farmer describes his wife's day in 1562.*

SOURCE B:
The inside of a country cottage.

Regardless of whether you were rich or poor at this time, having children was particularly dangerous. People didn't know that germs caused illness so women often gave birth in filthy conditions – dirty water, filthy rags, no disinfectant, and no antibiotics. Often babies died soon after they were born and one in every five births ended with the death of the mother.

Historians can find out a lot more about richer women, but being wealthy didn't always mean that their lives were a lot better than poorer women's. Read the following extracts from the diary of Samuel Pepys, the London gentleman whose diaries we looked at in the section on the Great Fire of London. His wife was called Elizabeth.

2 May 1663
'Slept until 7 o'clock, then up to my office. Argued with my wife about her not keeping the house clean. I called her a "beggar" and she called me a "prick louse". Got drunk after dinner.'
19 December 1664
'I was angry with my wife for not telling the servants what to do properly. She gave me an angry answer so I hit her over the left eye, such a blow as the poor wretch did cry out. She then scratched and bit me.'

SOURCE C: *From Samuel Pepys' diary.*

⏸ PAUSE for Thought

Historians know less about poorer women in Tudor and Stuart England than they do about richer women. Most of the poor couldn't read or write letters or keep diaries for us to study years later. However, richer women are easier to find out about. They wrote to friends, kept diaries, allowed themselves to be painted and sometimes earned so much money that they had to pay taxes – which were recorded of course.

A woman's life

Many women had their husbands chosen for them by parents and husbands had a lot of power over their wives. For instance, a 'nagging' wife could find herself on the **ducking stool**. She would be tied to a stool and lowered into the local pond as punishment. If that didn't work, she may even be forced to wear a **scold's bridle** for a day or so – an iron mask put over the woman's head, with a piece of metal that went into her mouth to hold her tongue down and stop her talking. The husband would then lead her around on a leash to show other men that he had her under control.

Women were not allowed to divorce their husbands but even if they could have done so, they wouldn't have been able to take any of their property with them. The law stated that once a woman was married, everything she owned became her husband's. Men, however, were allowed to divorce their wives. One kind of divorce was a **wife sale** in which men were allowed to sell off their wives.

SOURCE D: *A scold's bridle.*

WISE-UP Words

ducking stool
scold's bridle
spinsters
wife sale

! FACT Spinning sisters

Some women never got married. After Henry VIII closed the convents, they couldn't become nuns either. So some had to stay at home with their parents and spin wool to make a little money to live off. Even today, unmarried older women are called '**spinsters**'.

'He put a rope around her neck and led her to the market place. He puts her up to be sold to the highest bidder, as if she were a horse. A buyer is usually arranged beforehand.'

SOURCE E: *This description of a 'wife sale' was written in 1700.*

As you can see, many women lived tough lives but some visitors to this country thought differently. The writer of the following source thought that wealthy English women were still better off than women from other countries.

'Wives in England are in the power of their husbands, but they are not kept as strictly as in Spain. Nor are they shut up. They go to market, are well dressed. Some take it easy and leave the care of the household to their servants. They spend time walking and riding, playing cards and visiting friends, talking to neighbours and making merry with them, and [discussing] their childbirth and christenings. All this with the permission of their husbands. This is why England is called the paradise of married women.'

SOURCE F: *Written by a male visitor from Holland in 1575.*

Work

1 Write a sentence or two to explain the following:

ducking stool • scold's bridle • wife sale

2 Look at Source B.

a There are three people in the picture. What are they doing?

b Look at the woman cleaning clothes on the table. Describe the sort of day you think she was having. Use Source A to help you.

c How has cooking and washing changed since then?

3 a Why do you think one in five births ended with the death of the mother?

b How are conditions different today?

4 Read Source F.

a Do you think the visitor was describing the lives of rich or poor women? Give reasons for your answer.

b He describes England at this time as 'the paradise of married women'. Do you agree? Give reasons for your answer, using evidence from these pages.

5 Design a poster advertising a wife sale. With a partner or as a class, work together to decide what sort of information your poster needs to display.

+ Hungry for MORE

Read Source C again. It is from the diary of Samuel Pepys. Imagine that Elizabeth Pepys kept a diary too. Write her diary entries for 2 May and 19 December. She would probably have had a different view on the matter!

MISSION ACCOMPLISHED?

- Can you name two ways in which the life of a rich Stuart woman was different from a poor Stuart woman?
- Do you know how some women were treated by their husbands?

Have you been learning? 2

TASK 1 Source analysis

Some of our maids sitting up late last night to get things ready against our feast today, Jane called up about three in the morning, to tell us of a great fire they saw in the City. So I rose, and slipped on my night-gown and went to her window, and thought it to be on the back side of Mark Lane at the farthest; but, being unused to such fires as followed, I thought it far enough off, and so went to bed again, and to sleep.... By and by Jane comes and tells me that she hears that above 300 houses have been burned down tonight by the fire we saw, and that it is now burning down all Fish Street, by London Bridge. So I made myself ready presently, and walked to the Tower; and there got up upon one of the high places... and there I did see the houses at the end of the bridge all on fire, and an infinite great fire on this and the other side... of the bridge....

So down [I went], with my heart full of trouble, to the Lieutenant of the Tower, who tells me that it began this morning in the King's baker's house in Pudding Lane, and that it hath burned St. Magnus's Church and most part of Fish Street already. So I rode down to the waterside... and there saw a lamentable fire.... Everybody endeavouring to remove their goods, and flinging into the river or bringing them into lighters that lay off; poor people staying in their houses as long as till the very fire touched them, and then running into boats, or clambering from one pair of stairs by the waterside to another. And among other things, the poor pigeons, I perceive, were loth to leave their houses, but hovered about the windows and balconies, till they some of them burned their wings and fell down.

Having stayed, and in an hour's time seen the fire rage every way, and nobody to my sight endeavouring to quench it... I [went next] to Whitehall (with a gentleman with me, who desired to go off from the Tower to see the fire in my boat); and there up to the King's closet in the Chapel, where people came about me, and I did give them an account [that]dismayed them all, and the word was carried into the King. So I was called for, and did tell the King and Duke of York what I saw; and that unless His Majesty did command houses to be pulled down, nothing could stop the fire. They seemed much troubled, and the King commanded me to go to my Lord Mayor from him, and command him to spare no houses...

The extract above is from Samuel Pepys diary entry for 2 September 1666. Read the extract and then answer the following questions:

1 What historic event is Pepys describing?

2 How did Pepys first hear about the fire?

3 How did he first react to the news?

4 Where did Pepys go to get a good view of the fire?

5 According to Pepys, at what point did the poor people leave their houses?

6 What wildlife does Pepys describe suffering from the fire?

7 Who was Pepys taken to in order to describe the fire?

8 What was his reaction?

TASK 2 Anagrams

The following words are anagrams (words with their letters jumbled up). See if you can put the letters in the correct order to spell a word. Use the clues to help you:

a het begol – the name of the theatre where Shakespeare worked

b anmo sila – one of the most famous paintings in the world

c sncesaaneri – means rebirth

d sclomubu – sailed west in the Pinta, Nina and Santa Maria

e iamsaur – Japanese knights

f ermoo nad ljitue – famous lovers created by Shakespeare

g nisrttafodra – someone who believes William Shakespeare wrote the plays such as *Macbeth*, *A Midsummer Night's Dream* and *Hamlet*

h wne dlwro – what people called the land that Columbus discovered

i rmnaptsuci – anti-Stratfordians point out that there are none of these in Shakespeare's handwriting

j yokto – the capital city of the country where William Adams lived

TASK 3 Fact, opinion and punctuation

The following sentences have no capital letters, commas or full stops. Copy them out, adding the correct punctuation. Then underline the facts in blue and the opinions in red:

a king henry desperately wanted a son who could be king after him he must have hated his two daughters mary and elizabeth

b tudor schools were very strict you could be beaten for being late swearing gambling and forgetting books

c strolling players were groups of actors who travelled from village to village they were often joined by jugglers musicians and puppeteers

d despite queen elizabeth's attempts to keep her youthful looks she failed miserably she wore a wig because she was bald and had a mouthful of black teeth she was an ugly woman

e tudor women were probably all crazy to put harmful chemicals like sublimate of mercury on their faces it caused women's faces to flake like paint

f king philip of spain hated sir francis drake more than anyone else

g by 1568 elizabeth had been queen for ten years she hadn't married and she hadn't any children

h john hawkins was a cruel man who was responsible for shipping people as slaves to america

TASK 4 True or false?

Below are 12 sentences about the traditional story of the Gunpowder Plot – some of them are true and some are false. Correct the false ones and then place them all in the correct chronological order:

a The gang tried to tunnel under Parliament where the Queen was to sit.

b Lady Monteagle received a warning letter about a plot to kill the King.

c Thomas Casey rented a house next to Parliament.

d The cellars below Buckingham Palace were searched and a man by the name of John Johnson was found there. He was taken to the King.

e The tunnel plan failed when it filled with custard.

f The noise from the exploding gunpowder alerted the King's troops. After a shoot-out, killing Catesby and Percy, the remaining plotters were arrested.

g Percy then rented a cellar under Parliament. He smuggled in barrels of gunpowder and hid them behind piles of wood.

h The letter was taken to Robert Redford, the King's chief advisor, and then to the King.

i After a quick trial, the plotters, along with Guy Fawkes, were set free.

j John Johnson refused to answer the King's questions. He was taken to McDonald's and after 20 days of torture there, he revealed his real name – Guido Fawkes.

k The remaining plotters, aware that the plan had failed, barricaded themselves into Holbeach House in the Midlands.

Can you cure King Charles II?

MISSION OBJECTIVES

- To work through the various treatments on offer to sick King Charles II and make decisions about what to do.
- To understand why some of the choices were available during the Stuart period.

In Stuart times, approaches to medicine were a combination of different ideas. Some were very clever… but others were just crazy! Some doctors were beginning to work out exactly how the human body worked. Others hadn't got a clue! One of the most widely used cures was 'bloodletting'. This was based on an old Greek and Roman idea that too much blood in a person's body was the cause of their illness. The answer was to cut the patient and let out the 'bad blood'. Soon their body would be back 'in balance' again. Needless to say, it didn't work, but it didn't stop some of England's most famous doctors from trying it.

The King is ill

At 8:00am on 2 February 1685, Charles II fainted. It was soon clear that he was very ill. A dozen doctors gathered around his body. This was their chance to prove themselves as great doctors. If they could save him they would be richly rewarded. Fail and the King might die – and nobody wanted the blame for that!

Like all doctors, they had a choice of treatments. Imagine that you were one of the King's doctors. You will be given a series of choices to make based on real treatments available at the time.

Can you cure King Charles II?

What to do

1 Read each of the 'How's he feeling?' boxes carefully. They will give you some idea of the King's condition.

2 Choose a treatment from the list. You must have a good reason for your choice.

3 Record your choice and make a note of the reason.

Best of luck!

How's he feeling? 2 February

After collapsing, the King has been unconscious for two hours. As the doctors arrive, he begins to wake up. He is in pain.

Treatment 1: What do you do?

Do you:

a Open up a vein in his arm and drain 16oz of blood, then make him vomit?

b Do nothing and wait to see if he gets any better?

c Wash his hair in urine?

He's just as bad. You must keep trying.

Treatment 2: What will you do next?

Do you:

a Bleed him again, perhaps 8oz of blood from his shoulder this time?

b Shave his head and burn his scalp to make it blister?

c Pray?!

How's he feeling? 3 February

The King is speaking again but still feels poorly. He still faints occasionally but recovers sooner than the day before.

Treatment 3: What do you do?

Do you:

a Suggest injecting him with **antibiotics**?

b Drain more blood and then pump a liquid up his bottom to make him empty his bowels?!

c Leave him alone, he seems better today – perhaps he is getting well?

How's he feeling? 4 February

He wakes up bright and early but collapses again at dinner time. He seems to be getting worse.

Treatment 4: What do you do?

Do you:

a Bleed him again – more than you have already?

b Give him powdered human skull in a sweet drink? This is viewed by many as a super cure for any illness.

c Call another doctor; perhaps he can help more than you? Some people are saying that herbal remedies can work really well.

How's he feeling? 5 February

The King is getting worse. He collapses again. He sometimes cries out in pain. The doctors are very frustrated.

Treatment 5: What do you do?

Do you:

a Mash up the brain of a young man that has died violently, add some wine and horse dung and pour this over the King's body?

b Carry out more bleeding – perhaps give him a **laxative** to empty his bowels?

c Force him to eat Peruvian tree bark, a general medicine used for fevers?

↵ SOURCE A: *A picture of Charles II touching people to cure a common skin disease of the time known as 'King's evil'.*

WISE-UP Words

antibiotics
bloodletting
laxative

! FACT Doctors of death

Years later, it was discovered that the King had a kidney disease. The last thing that Charles needed was the bloodletting treatment. In fact, losing blood is the worst treatment a kidney patient can receive. His doctors actually shortened his life.

How's he feeling? 6 February

The King is still getting worse. The doctors think there is great danger that he may die. Perhaps there is one last chance?

Treatment 6: What do you do?

Do you:

a Cut his gums open with a new nail and then hammer the nail into an old oak tree?

b Give him some oriental Bezoar stone – this is a substance found in the stomachs of Persian goats? Added to wine, it should stop all poisons.

c Stop treating him; nothing you do seems to have any effect?

STOP PRESS ... STOP PRESS ... STOP PRESS ... STOP PRESS ...

The King is dead. Shortly after noon he collapsed for the last time. The doctors failed to keep him alive.

It is 1685 and the King has just died. All the doctors failed. But how did you perform? Would you have made a successful doctor in Stuart England?

SCORE CARD

Use this score chart to work out your points for the doctor task. When you have your final score, look at the 'How did you get on?' box and see if you would make a good Stuart doctor.

Treatment 1
a Yes, this is what the doctors did: 5 points.
b You must do something – you are one of the King's doctors – you can't just sit there: 0 points.
c Don't be silly, this is a Stuart cure for ringworm. It might be worth a try though!: 3 points.

Treatment 2
a This is what the doctors did. Bloodletting was the key to success... or so they thought: 5 points.
b The doctors did this too. Good thinking: 5 points.
c Not a bad idea, perhaps God would help him: 2 points.

Treatment 3
a Antibiotics? They'd never heard of them. Nobody knows what you are talking about – be careful, some people might think you are a witch!: 0 points.
b Good idea. This is what the King's doctors did: 5 points.
c Sounds sensible doesn't it? But you are missing a day's bleeding: 0 points.

Treatment 4
a Not a bad idea, but if you bleed too much you might put him 'out of balance' again: 3 points.
b This is what the doctors did: 5 points.
c Get another doctor! Don't be ridiculous. The King's doctors know what they are doing (even if he's not getting better!): 0 points.

Treatment 5
a A good treatment, but one for the plague. Perhaps worth a try though!: 3 points.
b Another good treatment, perhaps tomorrow?: 2 points.
c This is what the doctors did: 5 points.

Treatment 6
a A common treatment for toothache – I don't think the King has toothache, but you never know!: 2 points.
b This is what the doctors did: 5 points.
c You can't stop treating him, he's the King!: 0 points.

How did you get on?

If you scored 20 or more:
You would have made a very successful doctor in Stuart England. However, you may have killed a lot of patients!

11–19:
You would have made a good Stuart doctor. However, you've still got a lot to learn. Some of your treatments were clever, others were just crazy!

10 or below:
You would have failed as a Stuart doctor. You seem to know nothing about treating people. However, if the real doctors hadn't have taken so much blood, the King might have lived longer… read on.

Work ───────

1 Look at Source A.

a How did King Charles cure 'King's evil'?

b Why do you think so many people visited King Charles?

c By the mid 1700s, people stopped visiting the monarch to be cured of King's evil. What does this tell us about people's faith and its connection to medicine during this time?

── MISSION ACCOMPLISHED? ──

• Can you give three examples of treatments given to King Charles II and do you understand how his doctors may have contributed to his death?

How did people's thinking about the world change?

- To compare people's beliefs at the beginning and the end of the period 1500–1750.

In the Middle Ages (the time between 1066 and the Tudor period) there was a rebirth in learning, as some people began to question what had been accepted for centuries and started to investigate and experiment in science. Indeed the changes that took place in the 1600s have led some people to call it the 'scientific revolution'. But is this a good description? To answer this question, we need to study what many thought around 1500 and compare what they thought about the world by 1750. So what did people think in 1500?

The Middle Ages are often called the Age of Faith. Some people use this label because most ordinary men and women believed completely – and without question – in whatever the Church said. They thought that God controlled everything – for example whether there was a poor harvest or if your child died… and the best way to find out about the world they lived in was to study the Bible and attend church. But during the sixteenth and seventeenth centuries some people started to think deeply about religion and tried to find new answers about God and worship.

The universe

In 1500, most people thought that the Earth was at the centre of the universe and the Sun and the planets moved around it in circles. They thought the Sun and the planets were part of a heavenly world which was perfect. Source A sums up what people thought in 1500.

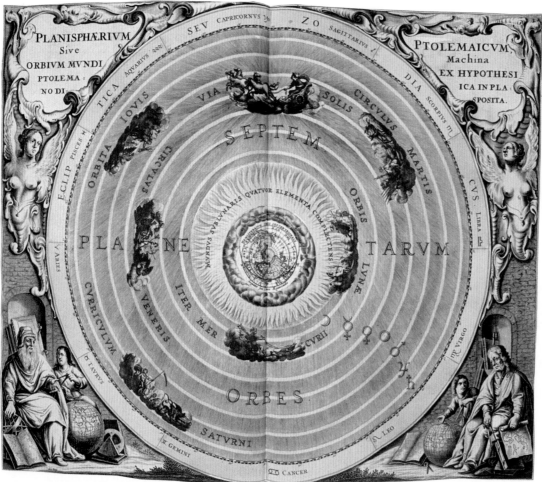

↵ SOURCE A: *Ideas about the universe were based on the theories of Ptolemy, who lived in the second century. This map, showing his theories, shows the Earth at the centre of the universe with the Sun and planets circling it.*

The Earth is the centre of the universe and God holds the answer to everything.

Science and Medicine

In 1500, doctors relied on ancient books written by Greek and Roman writers to tell them how the human body worked. There was some excellent advice in these books – but a lot of the fine detail was wrong. For example, in 1500 most still believed a 1000-year-old theory that new blood was constantly being manufactured in the liver to replace blood that was burned up in the body, like fuel. However, doctors didn't have much chance to correct these ancient theories because they were banned (by the Church) from cutting up dead bodies to find out what human insides looked like. Another key medical belief in 1500 was the theory of 'Four Humours'. The idea behind this was that the human body was made up of four substances, or 'humours' – blood, phlegm, yellow bile and black bile. They thought that illness was a result of the humours being 'out of balance'. For example, if a person had a fever, a doctor in 1500 might conclude that they had too much blood in their body, which was making them hot and wet. The doctor's solution would probably be to 'bleed' them. This meant opening up a vein and letting out some of their blood in order to put their body back in balance again! And there was even a chance that the equipment the doctors used to cut open the vein would have been filthy because doctors didn't know about germs and bacteria.

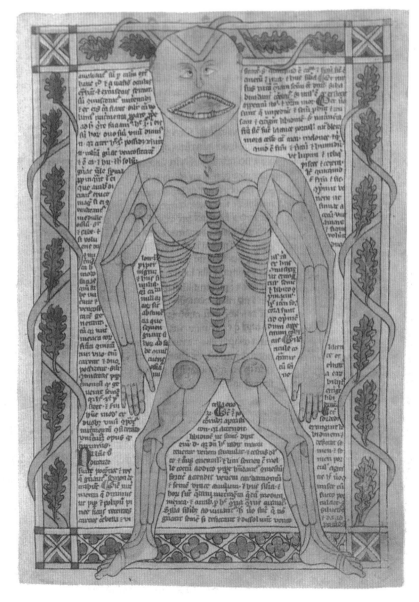

↵ **SOURCE B:** *A medieval drawing of the human body.*

1543 – Polish **astronomer** Nicolas Copernicus used mathematics to work out that the Sun – and not the Earth – was the centre of the universe. He proved that the Earth and all the other planets moved around the Sun… and that the moon moved around the Earth.

1543 – In Italy, a doctor called Vesalius published some of the first accurate drawings of the human body (see source D). He robbed cemeteries to get the bodies of executed criminals so he could study them and conducted experiments which proved some of the ancient medieval theories were wrong.

1575 – A French army surgeon, Ambroise Pare, used bandages and soothing ointments (rather than boiling oil) to treat wounds and prevent infection.

1600

1610 – An Italian, Galileo, made the first really practical telescope and saw for the first time planets such as Mars and Venus. However, when he said he could prove that the Earth moved around the Sun the Church rejected this idea… and made him deny his theory in public!

'The moon isn't smooth; its rough, full of cavities [holes], like the face of the earth.'

↳ **SOURCE E:** *Galileo 1610.*

1628 – English doctor, William Harvey, proved that the heart is a pump and circulates blood around the body (see Source F). Soon after, the doctors began to experiment with blood transfusions.

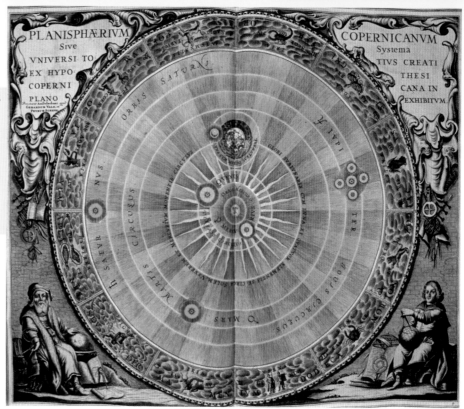

↳ **SOURCE C:** *The universe according to Copernicus. Note: i) the Sun at the centre; ii) the planets (inc. Earth) circling the Sun; iii) the Moon circling Earth; iv) the four planets circling Jupiter (Copernicus didn't know about these – they were first seen through a telescope in 1610); v) the signs of the zodiac around the edge of the map – many believed that the signs of the zodiac affected life on Earth in some way.*

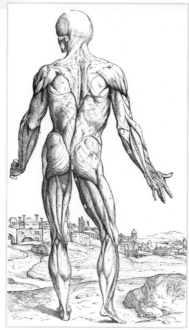

↳ **SOURCE D:** *An illustration from Versalius' book.*

SOURCE F: *A Harvey blood flow diagram from a book he wrote. By cleverly experimenting on the veins in people's arms, Harvey proved that the heart pumps blood around the body.* ↳

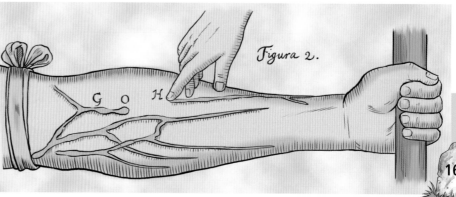

1650

134

WISE-UP Words

astronomer
inoculation

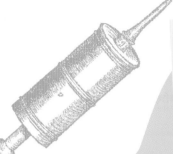

SOURCE G: *Isaac Newton on an old £1.00 note, which was used instead of £1 coins.* ↱

1686 – In London, Isaac Newton laid down the laws of gravity. 'Newton's Laws' are concerned with the way in which gravity acts on stars and planets – even today his methods are used to work out where stars will be at any given time.

1700

1705 – Astronomer Edmund Halley published a report stating that comet sightings in 1456, 1531, 1607, and 1682 related to the same comet. He predicted the comet's return in 1758 and when it was seen again it was called 'Halley's Comet'. The comet continued to appear every 75 or 76 years. It last appeared in 1986 and it is next due to appear in the summer of 2061.

1680 – Dutchman Antonie van Leeuwenhoek improved the basic microscope and was able to see blood in microscopic detail. He was the first to show that a droplet of water contained thousands of tiny living creatures.

1717 – Lady Mary Wortley experiments with smallpox **inoculations** (a way of preventing a person getting the disease). After the success of her experiments, King George I even had his own grandchildren inoculated!

1662 – The Royal Society was formed, backed by King Charles II. This group of scientists met regularly to discuss their ideas and experiments. Charles even increased the number of hanged criminals whose bodies were made available to doctors. This was the first group of its kind in the world and it still meets regularly today.

Work

1 a Why do you think the Middle Ages are sometimes called the 'Age of Faith'?

b Write down five things a person who lived in 1500 might think about the universe, science and medicine.

2 a Each of these dates is important in the history of science:

1680, 1682, 1662, 1686, 1717, 1543, 1655, 1705, 1575, 1610, 1661.

Write each date on a separate line in chronological order. Beside each date, write down the scientific invention or discovery that occurred during that particular year.

b Choose three developments and/or inventions from the timeline and explain how they made people healthier.

c Choose another three developments and/or inventions from the timeline and explain how they helped improve scientists' understanding of the world

1661 – In London, Robert Boyle proves that air is essential for both breathing and burning. He showed that all substances were made up of elements – and not a mixture of earth, air, fire and water, which is what people had believed since ancient times. Boyle is often called the father of modern physics.

3 a Historians sometimes call the period between 1500 and 1750 the 'scientific revolution'. What do you think is meant by this term?

b Do you think this is a suitable label? Explain your answer.

1655 – Dutchman Christian Huggens made big improvements in earlier telescopes and was able to see planets more clearly than ever before.

—MISSION ACCOMPLISHED?—

• Test your understanding of this section by explaining how three key individuals that you have just studied changed people's thinking about the world between 1500 and 1750?

WHO RULES?

When Charles II died in 1685, he left 14 children behind. Unfortunately, none of them were by his wife! No wonder he was called the 'Merry Monarch'! This meant that his children were illegitimate and therefore not able to inherit the Crown. The next in line for the throne was Charles' younger brother, James – and that was where the problem lay. So what was this problem? Who was against James becoming king? And what did James do make matters even worse?

1: The end of the Stuarts

MISSION OBJECTIVES

- To understand how the personal life of Charles II caused a crisis for Parliament.
- To know why some people didn't want James to become king.
- To understand what James did to make himself even more unpopular.

The Catholic conversion

While Charles II was still alive, James announced that he and his second wife had become Roman Catholics. As James was the heir to the throne, this caused a massive problem for Parliament. There hadn't been a Catholic monarch in England since 'Bloody Mary' and they were extremely worried about the Pope regaining control of Britain's religion. Others didn't object to James becoming king because they knew that his two daughters were Protestants. They were James' only children and would inherit the throne when he died.

I don't want a Catholic on the throne. What will happen to the Church of England?

James has the right to be king. He is an old man of 51 so the Crown will soon pass to his Protestant daughters – the future of the Church of England is safe.

SOURCE A: *The Stuart family tree.*

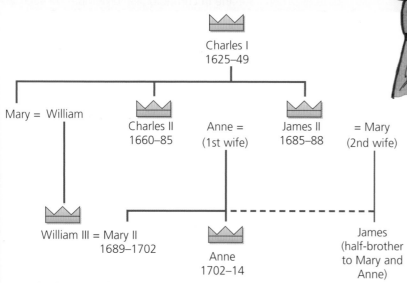

Charles I
1625–49

Mary = William   Charles II
1660–85   Anne =
(1st wife)   James II
1685–88   = Mary
(2nd wife)

William III = Mary II
1689–1702   Anne
1702–14   James
(half-brother to Mary and Anne)

King James II

With the support of Charles II, James won the argument. He promised to defend the Church of England, which is what most people were worried about, and was crowned king when his brother died.

As soon as James became king, the MPs that supported him started to think that they had made a big mistake. The new Catholic monarch made moves that alarmed everybody in Parliament. Look at the cartoons below and see if you can work out why.

WISE-UP Words

illegitimate

James used his power to over-rule the law that banned Catholics from the army and the government. Soon most of the top soldiers and politicians were Catholics.

James built up a large army – even though there wasn't a war on. Could he be planning to use this army against Parliament?

James claimed in a speech in 1687 that he thought 'all my subjects are members of the Catholic Church'. To many, this proved that James was planning to turn England Catholic!

In 1687, James lost patience with Parliament and closed it down. He was behaving exactly like his father Charles I – and we all know how that ended!

In 1688, the unthinkable happened! James' Catholic wife gave birth to a baby boy. As he was male, he pushed past James' daughters to be next in line for the throne!

This was too much for everybody in Parliament. The Catholic monarch was no longer a temporary thing. The new prince would be brought up a Catholic and so would his sons. England's kings would always be Catholics! Parliament decided to act.

Work

1 a Look at Source B. Why did some people support James' claim to the throne?

b Why did others object to James becoming king?

2 a Imagine you are a Member of Parliament in 1685 who supports James inheriting the throne. You are Protestant but don't mind the idea of a Catholic being king for a while. Write a letter to a friend explaining why you are not worried about the future of the Church of England (You might want to mention Mary and Anne!).

3 b Now imagine you are that same MP in 1688. Have you changed your mind? Write another letter to your friend explaining how and why your feelings about James have changed.

4 Which of James' actions upset Parliament the most? Copy the following sentences out into the order that you think would have caused the most alarm? Write a conclusion explaining why you have chosen the order you have.
- He dissolved Parliament.
- He gave all the top jobs to Catholics.
- He created his own army.
- His wife gave birth to a son.
- He claimed that all the people in England were Catholic.

MISSION ACCOMPLISHED?
- Could you explain why none of Charles II's children inherited the throne?
- Do you know what made Charles unpopular with some people in Parliament?
- Have you decided what made James even more unpopular?

In 1688, James I's wife gave birth to a healthy, male, Catholic baby. This meant that the English crown was destined to remain in Catholic hands. To some, it all seemed a bit too convenient for James. The Bishop of London even claimed that the Queen had never been pregnant at all and that the baby had been smuggled into the royal bed in a warming pan! The rich and powerful landowner MPs needed to act. They came up with a plan for someone to come and remove James II, and his son, from the throne. But who could do this? What was their claim to the throne? And who controlled the English crown at the end of the Glorious Revolution?

2: Would you invade our country please?

MISSION OBJECTIVES

- To be able to explain who Parliament turned to in order to prevent a permanent Catholic monarchy.
- To know how and why James II reacted to this invasion.
- To be aware who was on the English throne at the end of the Glorious Revolution.

Dastardly daughters!

Parliament looked to the King's own daughters for help. His eldest daughter, Mary, had been married off to a Dutchman called William of Orange when she was 15. They were both Protestants and William was already fighting a war against the Catholic King of France. The last thing he wanted was another neighbouring country to turn Catholic. When Parliament asked William to invade England and remove his father-in-law from the throne – he jumped at the chance!

⤴ SOURCE A: *William of Orange and his 12 000 troops sailed across the Channel from Holland to Torbay. They landed without resistance.*

The future's orange!

William landed on 5 November 1688 and quickly set off on the road to London. You might be expecting to hear horrific stories about how James' armies launched a massive attack leaving thousands dead and injured – but it didn't happen! Instead of rushing to face his invading son-in-law, James sat and waited as his most trusted general, John Churchill, and his other daughter, Anne, deserted him. It soon became clear that James didn't have the support to fight William's army. He decided to run for his life.

The Glorious Revolution

James escaped to France by boat with his wife and son. As he waved goodbye to London, he threw the Great Seal, needed for all official documents, into the Thames. He had given up the fight. There had been no bloodshed, no executions and no battles – but there had been a revolution! Parliament had acted to replace the ruler of the country – they called it the Glorious Revolution.

The Stuart see-saw of power!

James I claimed his power was given by God. Parliament kept him in check by controlling taxes. (1603–25)

Charles I dissolves Parliament and rules the country with absolute power! (1625–49)

The Civil War! Charles loses his head and Parliament rules England under the Commonwealth. (1649–60)

The Restoration! The 'Merry Monarch' Charles II is called home. (1660–85)

James II dissolves Parliament and rules with his Catholic advisors. (1685–88)

The Glorious Revolution! James II flees and Parliament regains control. They ask William and Mary to become king and queen – but under what conditions?

So Parliament had forced James II from power and had appointed a new king and queen – but this time it was on their terms! See what this meant for the future of the monarchy in Britain on the next page!

Work

1 Place the following events into the correct order and then draw a storyboard to illustrate them.
- William lands in Torbay with 12 000 troops.
- James flees London, throwing the Great Seal in the Thames.
- James' wife has a son.
- Rich politicians invite William to invade England.
- The King's daughter and the leader of his army run off to join William.

2 Imagine you are a Protestant plotter. Write a letter to William and Mary detailing your plan and asking them for their help. Give reasons for your actions and why you think your idea is a good one.

3 The 'Glorious Revolution' is sometimes called the 'bloodless revolution'. Why do you think it was given this other name?

4 Draw this puzzle in your book and fill in the answers to the clues:

1 There were two of them – one lost his head.
2 They ruled after the Tudors.
3 Another word for a king or queen.
4 The religion of James II.
5 Protestants thought it was 'Glorious'.
6 James II's youngest daughter.
7 William's wife.

Read down the crossword (clue 8). Write a sentence or two about this word.

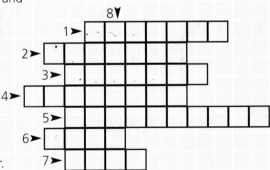

MISSION ACCOMPLISHED?

- Do you know who Parliament asked to remove James II from the throne?
- Could explain how James reacted to news of the invasion?
- Can you tell somebody who was king and queen at the end of the Glorious Revolution?

The Glorious Revolution meant that, once again, Parliament held the key to power in England. They had learned their lesson from Cromwell's commonwealth and decided that a new monarch was needed – but one that they controlled rather than one that controlled them. So how could they end the power struggles that had raged between the Crown and the People? What could they do to make sure they held on to power? And what did this mean for the future of the British monarchy?

3: The power of Parliament

MISSION OBJECTIVES

- To be able to explain the consequences of the Glorious Revolution.
- To know why the Stuart control of the English Crown ended and why it passed to a German man.

You can be queen as long as...

As she done so much to help remove her father from power, Parliament offered to make Mary the new Queen of England – but only under certain conditions. William wasn't willing to allow his wife to become queen alone, so Parliament extended the offer to both of them. William and Mary agreed to rule together – they also agreed to a few other things too!

PARLIAMENT

Makes **all** the new laws.

Controls all of the country's money.

Controls the Civil List – which states how much money the King gets every year.

Freedom of speech – they could say whatever they wanted – even about the King!

Freedom of press.

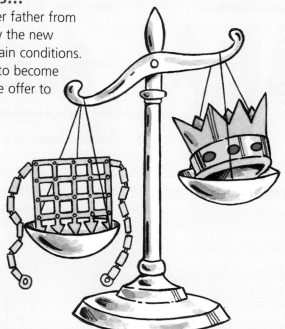

THE MONARCH

The monarch **had** to be a Protestant.

The King was not allowed his own, private army.

The King cannot interfere with trials.

The King cannot interfere in the running of Parliament.

The King must call Parliament.

The King has the power to appoint and dismiss Ministers and Lords.

Most of these agreements were made when William and Mary signed the **Bill of Rights** in 1689. There were also other changes made in 1694 when the **Triennial Act** was signed. This ensured that the monarch had to **consult** with Parliament and hold elections every three years. These changes set out the way the country has been run right up to the present day.

Power to the people?

Parliament justified taking the powers in the Bill of Rights because it said it spoke for the people. In reality, it only spoke for a few very rich people. Like today, Parliament had two houses: the House of Lords and the House of Commons. The aristocracy (Dukes and Earls and so on) sat in the House of Lords and other rich members of society were in the Commons. The Commons was **elected** but only a tiny proportion of men – and no women – had the vote. Those who could vote had to do it in public and so they were often **bribed** or forced to vote the way their landowner wanted. It took many more years of reform before Parliament represented everybody.

The final Stuart and German George

The Glorious Revolution and the Bill of Rights may have ensured Parliament's future – but it didn't do the same for the Stuarts. William and Mary both died childless so the crown passed to Mary's sister – who became Queen Anne in 1702. Anne had 11 children but all of them died tragically young. When she died in 1714, Parliament asked 'German George' to become king. Look at Source B and see if you if you can work out why Anne was the last Stuart monarch.

WISE-UP Words

Bill of Rights
bribed
consult
elected
Triennial Act

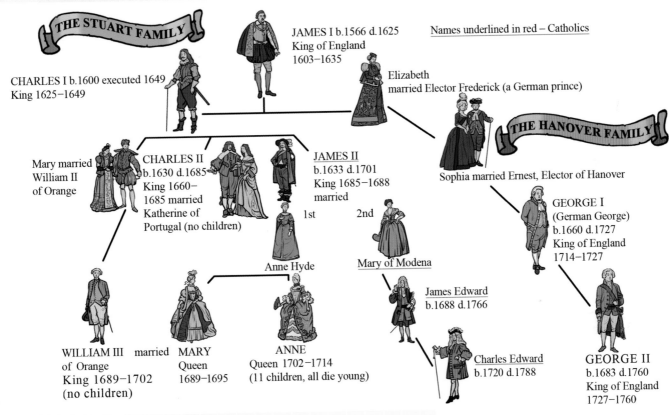

↰ SOURCE B: *The Stuart family tree.*

THE STUART FAMILY

JAMES I b.1566 d.1625
King of England
1603–1635

Names underlined in red – Catholics

CHARLES I b.1600 executed 1649
King 1625–1649

Elizabeth
married Elector Frederick (a German prince)

THE HANOVER FAMILY

Mary married William II of Orange

CHARLES II b.1630 d.1685 King 1660–1685 married Katherine of Portugal (no children)

JAMES II b.1633 d.1701 King 1685–1688 married

Sophia married Ernest, Elector of Hanover

1st

2nd

Anne Hyde

Mary of Modena

GEORGE I (German George) b.1660 d.1727 King of England 1714–1727

WILLIAM III of Orange King 1689–1702 (no children)

married

MARY Queen 1689–1695

ANNE Queen 1702–1714 (11 children, all die young)

James Edward b.1688 d.1766

Charles Edward b.1720 d.1788

GEORGE II b.1683 d.1760 King of England 1727–1760

Work

1 Copy the following statements into your book and decide if they are true or false:
   – The King could decide if people were guilty or innocent in trials.
   – The King couldn't keep his own army.
   – The King could decide on who ran the government.
   – Parliament controlled all of the country's money.
   – The King could overrule any decisions Parliament made.
   – Parliament was free to say whatever it wanted about the King.
   – The King could be Catholic or any other religion he chose.
   – The King had the right to stop newspapers writing nasty things about him.

2 Who do you think had the most power after the Glorious Revolution – the monarch or Parliament? Write a paragraph explaining your answer.

3 Why do you think William and Mary agreed to sign the Bill of Rights? Do you think Mary's father would have agreed to Parliament's demands?

4 Write one sentence explaining why Parliament turned to 'German George' when Queen Anne died childless.

___ MISSION ACCOMPLISHED? ___

• Could you explain three ways in which Parliament increased its power after James II was removed from the throne?

• Can you explain why they made these changes?

• Do you understand why the English crown was given to George, elector of Hanover?

Queen Anne was the last Stuart monarch. Thirty years later, a Scottish army was once again ready to launch an invasion of England. So who led this invasion? How did the people in England react? And which side won the last battle ever to be fought on British soil?

4: The Battle of Culloden

MISSION OBJECTIVES

- To be able to explain who Bonnie Prince Charlie was and why he tried to remove George II from the throne.
- To understand why many people in Scotland supported him.
- To know what was special about the Battle of Culloden.

When Queen Anne died, she left no children, brothers or sisters to replace her and power passed to George I. Not everybody was happy when the Crown passed to 'German George'. Scotland and England were separate countries but they shared the same monarch. This wasn't a problem when Charles II was alive but many in Scotland were deeply unhappy about the Glorious Revolution and James II's removal.

The Jacobites

People who supported James II and his descendants were known as Jacobites – from the Latin word for James – Jacobus. Most Jacobites came from Scotland, particularly the Highland clans. This is because they were Catholics, like James and his sons. They called James II's son 'the King over the water' – as he had been exiled to France and swore loyalty to him. By 1745, the Jacobites believed that they had the money, the support and the leader to put the Stuarts back in control.

Bonnie Prince Charlie

Charles Edward Stuart was the Grandson of James II and son of James Edward Stuart – the so-called 'Bed-Pan Baby'. He had gathered support for his struggle in Scotland and France and, on 19 August 1745, he snuck across the water. The Highland clans flocked to support him and 'Bonnie Prince Charlie' – as he became known – was soon marching with his army towards Edinburgh. He won a famous

Bonnie Prince Charlie.

victory at the Scottish capital and soon, all of Scotland was under his control. Bonnie Prince Charlie's advisors told him to stay north of the border and strengthen his position but he had other ideas. He would not rest until his father was sat on the English throne.

London calling

Charles was certain he would be joined by thousands of English Catholics. However, by the time he had reached the city of Derby, it had become clear that the support was not going to arrive. Only 300 English supporters had joined his army and none of them were wealthy or important. The Highlanders began to feel uncomfortable being so far away from home. Without reinforcements, they didn't see how they could take London. With heavy hearts, Bonnie Prince Charlie and his troops turned around and headed back for Scotland.

The chase to Culloden

If only the Bonnie Prince had known what was happening in London. The city was gripped by panic and King George II had packed his bags. When news came of Charles' retreat, there was incredible relief. George was not prepared to go through that again and sent his son, the Duke of Cumberland, to hunt down Bonnie Prince Charlie. On 16 April 1746, the Duke of Cumberland forced a showdown at Culloden.

Britain's last battle

The Duke of Cumberland's army was well armed and well trained. The Jacobites were exhausted and had been without food for three days – they had been waiting on Culloden Moor while Cumberland and his men had been celebrating his birthday! The Jacobites were outnumbered two to one, poorly armed and half-starving. When the killing stopped, 1200 Jacobites were left dead compared to only 76 of Cumberland's men.

⤴ SOURCE A: *People think of the Battle of Culloden as a battle between Scotland and England but there were more Scots fighting for the Duke of Cumberland than for Bonnie Prince Charlie.*

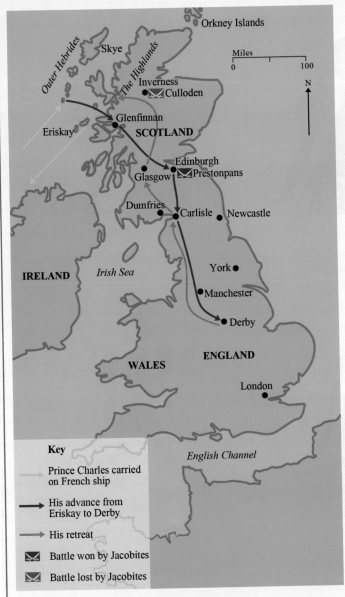

Key

- Prince Charles carried on French ship
- His advance from Eriskay to Derby
- His retreat
- Battle won by Jacobites
- Battle lost by Jacobites

! FACT Cumberland the butcher

Unfortunately for the Scots, the killing didn't end at Culloden. Cumberland headed for the Highlands in search of Bonnie Prince Charlie. The Highlanders were harshly treated and even banned from wearing tartan! The Bonnie Prince was never captured and lived for another 42 unhappy years abroad saying, 'I should have died with my men at Culloden.' He is still regarded as a hero by many in Scotland today, while Cumberland is widely hated for his cruel methods.

Work

1 Write a sentence explaining why the supporters of the Stuarts were called the Jacobites.

2 Why do think the Jacobites turned back when they reached Derby?

3 What do you think would have happened if they had carried on to London? Explain your answer carefully.

4 Name one thing that makes the Battle of Culloden significant.

5 Which of the following statements is more accurate?
   – The Jacobite invasion was England versus Scotland.
   – The Jacobite invasion was Catholics versus Protestants.

Explain your choice carefully.

—— MISSION ACCOMPLISHED? ——

- Could you explain to someone why Bonnie Prince Charlie invaded England in 1745?
- Do you know why many people in the Highlands supported his invasion?
- Can you tell someone who won the Battle of Culloden and what makes it so important in British history?

How did Britain change between 1485 and 1750?

MISSION OBJECTIVES

- To understand how Britain changed between 1485 and 1750.
- To remember at least five important ideas and inventions during this time.

This book covers the years 1485 to 1750. During this time, some amazing and lasting changes took place. New ideas and discoveries altered the way people looked at the world, whilst new inventions changed the way people did things. Read this section carefully. It doesn't feature all the changes, discoveries and inventions that took place between 1485 and 1750 but it tries to pick out some of the most important and interesting ones.

1485 – The beginning of the Tudor period.	**1603** – When Tudors became Stuarts.	**1750** – Long live the Georgians!
King and Parliament		

United Kingdom		

Two kings, one for England, one for Scotland, different parliaments.	King of England is also King of Scotland, different parliaments.	One king, one parliament for England, Scotland, Ireland and Wales.

1485	1603	1750

Population

1485	1603	1750
England 2.25m, Wales 0.2m, Scotland 0.5m, Ireland 0.8m. **3.75 million**	England 4–5m (approx.); Ireland, Scotland and Wales made up a further 2m of Britain's overall population (approx.). **6–7 million**	England and Wales 6.25m, Scotland 1.25m, Ireland 3.25m, British settlers overseas 3.0m. **13.75 million** (including 3m living abroad)

London – Britain's largest city

  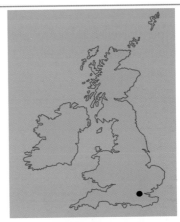

40 000 people	225 000 people	650 000 people

Religion

Everyone Catholic.	Most people are Church of England (Protestant). Catholics and pilgrims persecuted.	Most people Church of England (Protestant). Other religions are supposed to be free, but some restrictions still apply!

Communication

Mainly word of mouth.	Printed books and some newspapers (called broadsheets) are available but expensive.	First newspapers and magazines.

145

1485	1603	1750
Transport		

The rich travelled by horse (and carriage) the poor walked.	Richer men and women still travelled by horse and carriage – and the poor still walked.	Still horses and carriages and walking! There were 'sedan chairs' in the towns though (an early type of taxi).
Food and drink		

Beer, wine, cheese, meat, bread, vegetables, knives and spoons.	Beer, wine, cheese, meat, bread, more vegetables, salad, tobacco, knives and spoons.	Beer, wine, tea, coffee, drinking chocolate, cheese, meat, bread, more vegetables, potatoes, bananas, coconuts, salad, tobacco, knives, forks and spoons.
The known world		

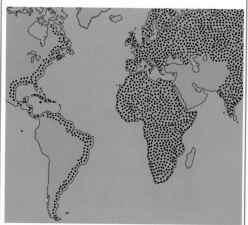

1485	1603	1750

Popular entertainment

Hunting, jousting, fighting games and blood sports.

Going to the theatre, blood sports and mob football.

Horse racing, cricket, blood sports and mob football.

Science and medicine

The Earth is the centre of the universe and God holds the answer to everything.

Very little known about science and the human body.

More understanding of Earth's place in the universe. Better knowledge of human body due to more accurate drawings. Improved treatment of war wounds.

Lots more known about chemistry, physics, biology and the universe. Didn't really help people stay alive longer but did bring about new ways of thinking.

Law and order

Stocks, pillory, whipping, execution common – but fines remain the most popular type of punishment. No police force.

Older forms of punishment still used. Torture common to get confessions. 'Witch hunting' set to become a craze! No police.

Savage punishments and many executions. Prisons used more for punishment as well. Bow street runners introduced, the beginnings of a police force.

Work

1 Produce a poster, a leaflet or an essay that both demonstrates and explains at least eight key ways in which Britain in 1485 was different to Britain in 1750.

2 In your opinion, what changed the most, and the least, between 1485 and 1750? Give reasons for your choices.

—MISSION ACCOMPLISHED?—

- Can you recall five facts about Britain in 1485 and five about Britain in 1750?

Have you been learning? 3

TASK 1 The Tudor family tree

Study the Tudor Family tree carefully – it is one of the best-known family histories in the world – and then answer the questions below.

a Can you remember why it was a good political move for Henry VIII to marry Elizabeth of York?

b How many children did Henry VII have?

c Why do you think Henry VII got his children to marry people from other Royal families in Europe?

d Why did Henry VIII marry Catherine of Aragon?

e Who was Henry VIII married to for the longest time?

f To which wife was he married to for the shortest amount of time?

g Write down the order in which Henry VIII's children were born, starting with the oldest.

h Write down the order in which Henry VIII's children became king or queen, starting with the first.

i Why did Henry's children not become monarch in the order in which they were born?

j According to the family tree, by the time Elizabeth became Queen (in 1558), who stood to inherit the throne after Elizabeth's death?

k When Elizabeth died in 1603, who became the next monarch?

TASK 2 Vowels and consonants

Complete the following famous people's names from your study of 1485–1750. Some of the names have missing vowels, others have missing consonants.

Look at the clues and write out the words, making sure you fill in the missing letters.

a _L_Z_B_ _H _F YO_ _
(Henry VII's wife)

b P_I_ _E_S E_I_A_ET_
(Her father was absent from her christening)

c A_ _E O_ CL_ _E _
(Divorced)

d W_LI_ _ _H_ _ES_ _A_E
(Inventor of new words)

e _E_NA_ _O D_ V_ _C_
(He wanted to know everything)

f JO_ _ H_W_ _NS
(A slave trader)

g _ _A_KBE_R_
(A scary man)

h _AR_ _UE_ _ O_ _C_TS
(A pain in the neck for Elizabeth)

i A_ _H_NY BA_I_ _T_N
(Hatched a secret plan to kill the Queen)

j K_ _G _A_ES
(England and Scotland)

k _L_VE_ _RO_W_ _L
(Not a friend of Charlie)

l _U_EN A_ _E
(The last Stuart)

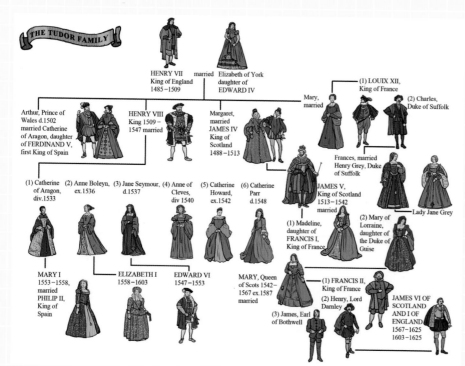

THE TUDOR FAMILY

HENRY VII
King of England
1485–1509
married
Elizabeth of York
daughter of
EDWARD IV

Arthur, Prince of Wales d.1502 married Catherine of Aragon, daughter of FERDINAND V, first King of Spain

HENRY VIII
King 1509–1547 married

Margaret, married JAMES IV King of Scotland 1488–1513

Mary, married
(1) LOUIX XII, King of France
(2) Charles, Duke of Suffolk

(1) Catherine of Aragon, div.1533
(2) Anne Boleyn, ex.1536
(3) Jane Seymour, d.1537
(4) Anne of Cleves, div 1540
(5) Catherine Howard, ex.1542
(6) Catherine Parr d.1548

JAMES V, King of Scotland 1513–1542 married

Frances, married Henry Grey, Duke of Suffolk

Lady Jane Grey

(1) Madeline, daughter of FRANCIS I, King of France
(2) Mary of Lorraine, daughter of the Duke of Guise

MARY I
1553–1558, married PHILIP II, King of Spain

ELIZABETH I
1558–1603

EDWARD VI
1547–1553

MARY, Queen of Scots 1542–1567 ex.1587 married

(1) FRANCIS II, King of France
(2) Henry, Lord Darnley
(3) James, Earl of Bothwell

JAMES VI OF SCOTLAND AND I OF ENGLAND 1567–1625 1603–1625

↵ SOURCE A:
The Tudor family tree.

TASK 3 Freeze frames

Imagine that you are watching a video film of the events in history that you have been studying. Someone has pressed 'pause' and frozen the picture. In groups, pretend that you are characters from history captured in the 'freeze frame'. When you have worked with your group to produce a freeze frame, why not show the remainder of your class and see if they can guess the event that you have chosen.

Here are some events that you could 'freeze':

- the execution of Guy Fawkes;
- the Great Plague;
- the execution of King Charles;
- the Great Fire of London;
- one of Henry VIII's divorces;
- the attack of the Spanish Armada;
- an event from the story of 'Blackbeard';
- the English Civil war;
- a witch trial;
- the discovery and colonisation of North America.

TASK 4 And now for the news!

The first daily newspaper didn't appear in England until 1702. Before then, information travelled by word of mouth, expensive printed books or by broadsheet – a large, single sheet of paper containing details of major events.

Try to imagine that there were daily newspapers throughout Tudor and Stuart times. Here are a few headlines you might have seen:

- 1537: Eddie's here!
- 1588: The bigger they come, the Armada they fall.
- 1605: Fawkes fails.
- 1649: Cromwell's crew chop Charlie.
- 1665: It's back!
- 1666: Inferno.

a Write a sentence or two explaining each headline.

b In small groups, write a newspaper article about each of the headlines. You could add some of your own headlines and stories. Your work could make an interesting class display.

TASK 5 Word grid

Use the clues below to complete this word grid.

1 What religion were the Jacobites?

2 The surname of Bonnie Prince Charlie.

3 The name of the Duke who won the Battle of Culloden.

4 The soft ground may have slowed this part of the Duke's army down.

5 Charles Edward Stuart's nickname.

6 The name of the English city reached by the Jacobites before they turned back.

7 The name of the followers of the Stuarts.

8 The capital city of Scotland.

149

Glossary

Adulterous An adulterous person is a married man or woman who is not faithful to their wife or husband.

Allies Two groups on the same side. Friends in battle.

Antibiotics A chemical substance used to destroy bacteria.

Anti-Stratfordian Someone who doubts that Shakespeare really wrote the plays attributed to him.

Architect A designer of buildings.

Armada A fleet of warships.

Astronomer A person who studies stars, planets and other bodies of the universe scientifically.

Belladonna A chemical used by Tudor women to make their eyes shine and sparkle.

Besieged Surrounded by armed forces.

Bill of Mortality A weekly list of the causes of death in a particular place.

Bill of Rights The agreements made between William and Mary and Parliament in 1689.

Birch A bundle of twigs tied together and used to hit children as a punishment. A cane was a single piece of wood.

Blasphemy Disrespect for God or other sacred things.

Blood sports Sports that involve cruelty to animals.

Bloodletting The practice of making someone bleed to cure an illness.

Bludgeoned Hit or beaten with a club.

Bribe Something, usually money, given to a person to influence their actions.

Bubonic One type of plague, named after one of its symptoms – buboes or boils.

Canting A secretive street language used by sturdy beggars.

Catholic A follower of the Catholic religion, one of the main Christian religions.

Cavaliers Nickname for the King's soldiers during the English Civil War.

Cavalry Soldiers on horseback.

Censored Banned or removed.

Citizen A person who lives in a town.

Civil war A war between two groups of people in the same country.

Class A group in society with the same economic or social status.

Cochineal A red dye or colouring, obtained from insects.

Colony An area of land in a new country occupied by people who still remain under the rule of their homeland.

Consult To ask someone for their advice or opinion.

Contemporary Something from the same period of time.

Convert To change, for example, your religion.

Corruption When something or someone is affected by bribery or another bad practice.

Cuckolding Being a married man but having 'affairs' with married women was called cuckolding in Tudor England.

Cudgelling A painful game involving hitting your opponent.

Death warrant A piece of paper ordering someone's execution.

Dissolution The act of officially breaking up an organisation. It is the word used to describe the time when Henry VIII closed all the monasteries in England and Wales.

Divine Right The belief that kings and queens could do as they wished because they were appointed by God.

Ducking stool A punishment for 'unruly' wives.

Elected Selected for a position by voting.

Enslavement To make slaves of people.

Excommunicated Expelled from the Catholic Church. A very serious religious punishment.

Execution The process of killing or beheading an enemy or convicted criminal.

Extremist A supporter of extreme measures (often political or religious).

Fire mark Displayed on the outside of people's houses to prove that their insurance fees had been paid.

Galleon A large warship.

Gallery A place to sit in a theatre.

Gallows The framework upon which guilty criminals were hanged.

Gangster A member of a criminal gang.

Genius A person with great ability.

Gentlemen Rich men, often dukes, earls or lords. They often own a lot of land.

Glorious Revolution The overthrow of James II by Parliament (led by William III) in 1688.

Grammar school A school that taught mainly Latin and Greek grammar.

Hornbook A flat, double-sided paddle, shaped like a table-tennis bat. Used to help students read and write.

House of Correction Criminals and people who refused to work were sent here. They then had to make things that were later sold.

Imported Brought in from another country, usually by boat.

Independent Free from the control of another country.

Indulgences You could 'buy' these from a bishop. They helped a person pass through purgatory more quickly.

Infantry Foot soldiers.

Inoculation A way of preventing a person getting a disease by introducing a small amount of it into their body, making them immune to it.

Laxative A medicine used to help a person go to the toilet easily.

Lenient Showing mercy or tolerance.

Malaria A disease spread by mosquitoes.

Merchant A person whose job is to buy and sell goods in order to make a profit.

Mercy showing understanding or kindness, especially to your enemy.

Musket A gun.

Musketeer A soldier who carries a musket.

Native Americans The tribesmen who have lived on the continent of North America for thousands of years. Sometimes incorrectly called 'Red Indians' or 'Redskins'.

Natives Members of the original race of a country. They were born there and have not been brought there by people.

Obituary Briefly tells of some of the most important events, achievements and the personality of a person who has recently died.

Parliamentarian A supporter of Parliament during the English Civil War.

Pauper Someone with no job. They rely on charity.

Persecution Extreme harassment of a person, often because of their religious or political beliefs.

Pike A long pole, tipped with a steel spike. Used as a weapon.

Pikeman A soldier who carries a pike.

Pilgrim Fathers The name given to the first Puritan settlers in America in 1620.

Pit The standing area nearest the stage in a theatre.

Playwright A person who writes plays.

Plundering Taking goods by force.

Poor Law A law passed in 1601 that placed paupers into four categories; each group was treated differently.

Pope The leader of the Catholic Church, who lives in Rome.

Population All the people who live in a particular place.

Printing press A machine used to print books.

Propaganda False or misleading information used to spread a certain point of view.

Purgatory The place between heaven and hell. A person is believed to be punished in purgatory for any sins they have committed on earth while alive.

Puritan A strict Protestant who wanted to worship God very simply.

Quill pen A pen made from feather. Dipped in ink to write.

Rabbi A Jewish priest.

Recusants Catholics refusing to accept the authority of the Church of England.

Reformation The name used to describe the changes or reforms made to the Catholic Church in the sixteenth century, mainly by Henry VIII and his son, later King Edward VI.

Regicide The official word for killing a king or queen.

Religious Settlement Made by Elizabeth in order to keep the peace between Catholics and Protestants as far as possible.

Renaissance The period between the fourteenth and sixteenth centuries in Europe when there was a rebirth in art, literature and learning.

Ridicule To make fun of someone in an unkind way.

Roundheads Nickname for Parliament's soldiers during the English Civil War.

Routine An established pattern of behaviour that people follow almost all the time.

Royalist A supporter of the King during the English Civil War.

Sash A coloured strip of cloth used to identify soldiers in battle.

Scold's bridle An iron mask put over a woman's head to stop her talking; used as a punishment.

Searcher Someone who looked for dead bodies or plague victims during the Great Plague of 1665.

Sedition Ordinary citizens disputing a king or queen's decisions.

Settler Somebody who moves to an area that was previously uninhabited or unknown.

Sewer A drain to remove waste water and sewage.

Shin-hacking A painful game involving kicking your opponent.

Ship tax A charge, introduced by Charles I, for people living by the sea.

Shorthand A type of coded writing that can be written quickly.

Sphere Ball shaped.

Spinster An unmarried older woman.

Stillborn A baby born dead.

Stratfordian Someone who believes that Shakespeare was responsible for writing the plays attributed to him.

Strolling players A group of travelling actors, musicians and entertainers.

Sturdy beggars Criminals who used clever tricks to get money.

Superstitious A belief in omens and ghosts. For example, the fear of the number 13.

Symbol Sign or thing that stands for something. For example, a cross is a symbol of Christianity.

Symptoms Signs of illness or disease.

Synagogue Jewish place of worship.

Tithes A type of tax; peasants had to give 10% of their harvest to the priest every year.

Treason A crime against a king or queen.

Triennial Act An agreement signed in 1694 ensuring that the monarch had to consult with Parliament and hold elections every three years.

Tuberculosis A lung disease.

Vagabond A wanderer or tramp.

Voyage A journey.

Wife sale A type of divorce. In Tudor and Stuart England, it was possible to sell your wife at a 'wife sale'.

Yeoman A farmer – some were rich; others were poor.

Index